A Pair of Gringos

Walking across Spain on the Camino de Santiago, Living Our Bucket List

Talking with GOD on the Camino he told me to SHUT UP, SLOW DOWN.. and other lessons learned along The Way... -Molli Rathstone

30 days,
over 200 photos
a day by day account of our trip
and what happened along The Way!

Instead of doing Acknowledgments I would like to offer my Apologies:

I would like to apologize, in advance, to Ms. Molumphy and all English teachers out there, whom I adore, for the grammatical errors within this text. I wrote it like I speak and I don't speak that well either...

Hope you can manage to overlook it and enjoy!

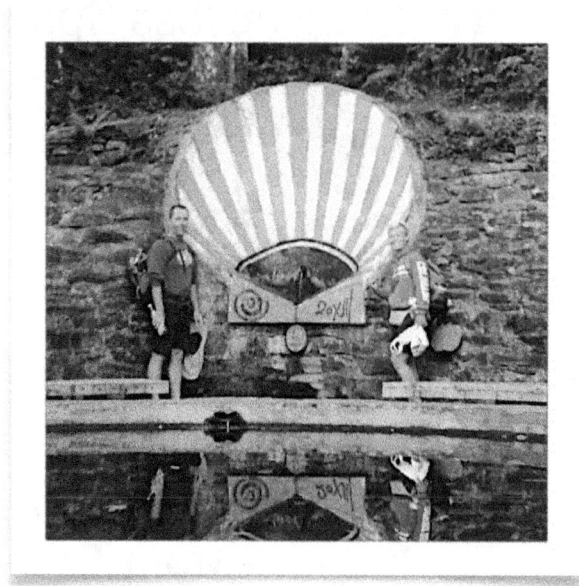

Disclaimer: Although every attempt has been made to provide accurate information, in this book, it is not intended to be used as a guidebook. Absolutely no guarantee is made regarding its accuracy. Reader assumes all responsibility and liability for any actions taken in relation to using the information provided within. This is our story and is not intended to be used as a guidebook.

All photographs by © Molli & Tony Rathstone

Table Of Contents:

How the Blog was Born or Pre-Camino

Once we made the decision to walk the Camino we began voraciously reading, in preparation.

We read Guidebooks such as John Brierley's, *A Pilgrim's Guide to the Camino de Santiago*. I thanked him, in my mind, every day for writing his Guide book... I found it invaluable how he combined so much of the necessary info any, good pocket, guidebook should contain and somehow managed to weave in so much heart. I mean truly if a guidebook could be a work of art, his is.

Anna Dintaman and David Landis', *A Village to Village Guide* to *Hiking the Camino de Santiago*... (I found it helpful to have two different guide books)

And several other novels, journals, blogs... and I am thankful for each in their own right.

In reading these accounts I began to very much appreciate the authors for opening themselves up and sharing their experiences. I learned an important lesson while reading them; just because you may disagree with the author's actions, grammar, thoughts, opinions or decisions does not mean you won't appreciate them for having shared their journey with you.

As I began reading one of the books, in particular, I was so bored by the authors style of writing, I could barely force myself to finish the book but by the end, I was in tears and so appreciative of him for having shared it!

This taught me what a man I have a lot of respect for, Larry Crane, means when he says "your opinion of me is none of my business"...

This realization gave me the courage to go ahead and share liberally our journey because no matter what your opinion of me and my writing it does not mean you won't appreciate us having shared it.

and so I took a deep breath and knew it was my responsibility, part of my journey to chronicle these events.

This is our story of what happened on the Camino Frances and how our lives have been radically changed as a result of walking it...

I did my best to be open and honest about our journey... and In looking back now I am very glad we kept the blog. It made us feel very connected to our friends and family at home and they reported back to us that they felt like they were with us on the journey. They loved it!

We have included the blog just as they saw it, day by day in this book, and we have added all of the takeaways we have experienced since coming home from the Camino. There have been many.

It's been a wild ride and we're glad to have you along as the journey continues.

Ultreia! Onto the next chapter...

Where the name Pair of Gringos came from...

When you're hiking the Camino you're called a "pilgrim" and the Spanish word for pilgrim is *Peregrino*.

Tony and I were practicing our Spanish and trying to do word association to remember "Peregrino" and we started cracking up that it sounds like a "Pair of Gringos" (which is exactly what we are, two dorks who can't speak a lick of Spanish!) so that's how the name came about.

"Hey we're a pair of gringos and peregrinos... Cool!" and so our blog's name was born:

www.Pair of Gringos.com

Our blog is still up, as is our *pair of gringos* facebook page, there you will find many more COLOR PICTURES and VIDEOS, of our journey, for you to Enjoy!

B.C. or Before our Camino

We decided to start posting content on the blog prior to leaving. The next several sections of this book are posts of the days leading up to our trip. These days were some of the most stressful I have experienced and I felt very much alone. Friends and family couldn't empathize with the logistics of what was going on. To them I'm sure all they saw was "Hey you get to go away for a month... You're so lucky" and my husband is a pretty laid back dude, not much rattles him. I on the other hand am not so laid back.

Let me give you an example to put the stress level I was experiencing into context. I have sold the entire contents of a 3400 sqft house, bought a motor home and moved into it in under 2 months time (about the same amount of time we gave ourselves to prepare for the Camino). That experience was a cake walk compared to this.

I don't mean to say you will have the same struggles, in fact, I have heard many accounts of people just getting up and leaving but for me this was not the case.

The Camino had called to us... I could feel that much and we were going... but the logistics of setting it up. The thought of leaving our dogs. The uncertainty of the whole thing was a very difficult process for me. I had a hard time getting into a peaceful place, mentally, during this time and was quite disappointed in myself for not being able to get to that "quiet" place which I know to be so important, for success, in any endeavor.

I knew if we made it to the Camino the hardest mountain would already have been conquered.

The first major climb had begun and it was my duty to push on...

When God calls, you go.

Ultreia!

Why the Camino... ?

In my reading I found, the Camino is important to the Christian religion because the bones of St. James are believed to be buried in the city of Santiago de Compostela however it is not only significant in the Christian religion.

The history of this path is immense. Over the course of time many religions and cultures have deemed it an important route which is why I find it so fascinating! I am very much looking forward to feeling what's different about this area of the world?

Why has this walk drawn so many people?

Over 200,000 people (pilgrims) per year take on this 500 mile walk. Why has this walk been so important to so many cultures and religions, from ancient times when pilgrims literally risked their lives to make the journey, until now, modern day?

How does it continue to draw people from behind their desks and away from their comfortable lives to take on such a physical feat? I can't wait to find out and I look forward to sharing the journey with you here on this blog. I feel writing this blog and being brutally honest with what I'm / we're experiencing along the way is a way I can give back and share the journey with you.

Maybe reading about our journey will be the catalyst for your next grand adventure... ! We certainly hope so. We love to inspire people to live out their dreams. Most of the time it will mean getting a little (or a lot) uncomfortable but we find it's ALWAYS worth it in the end. Life is meant to be lived... So here we go!

Why Now?

I turned 40 this year and Tony (my husband) turned 50. (2015)

We were trying to come up with something really cool to celebrate the year. So one afternoon Tony takes off to the book store (A favorite past time of his: To spend a couple hours just browsing the books).

He comes home and mentions a book which looks interesting, about the Camino, **Walking Home,** by Sonia Choquette.

We have both talked about, The Camino, being something we wanted to experience but it was nothing more than a "bucket list" item. No real plans... So he mentions this book and something just goes off inside me, a switch is flipped, and I knew we had to go get that book!

The next day we went back and purchased the book and while driving home we started reading it to each other (another past time, we love reading to each other while driving).

I don't think we got through the first chapter before we both looked at each other and **knew** ...

We were going to be walking the Camino and we were going to be walking it NOW!

This is how simply our journey began (and a glimpse into how spontaneous we are)...

2 and a half months later, our flights are booked, bags are packed, and we leave in 19 days...

Clueless on the Camino

I considered calling our blog *Clueless on the Camino* because going into this adventure, that's how I felt, Clueless... on many levels...

Clueless because no matter how hard I've tried, over the years, I have failed to retain any of the Spanish I have been taught. Many times on the Camino you are in rural villages where you are well advised to know and speak the language but I do not.

My joke is "My Spanish looks shockingly like charades". Clueless because you can't (or rather I should say we have decided not to pay to) book our rooms in advance... So I can't make myself feel more at ease by planning, double checking, triple checking and quadruple checking myself into infinity. On the Camino, many people believe, you are meant to "wing it", not plan in advance, and allow the Camino to take care of you.

Clueless check two-

Clueless because although deeply spiritual I AM NOT RELIGIOUS (I know that's about the most vapid and cliché term I could use but sorry it's true). I think I spend the better part of my day attempting to make sense as to why we are on this planet but I do not --prescribe- to any religion. Because the Camino is soaked in religion I will have to give myself checkmark #3 for being Clueless on the religious front.

Clueless because well the whole thing is completely insane! Who in their right mind; leaves work, to fly to a Country you've never been and walk 500 miles across it? Believing you'll be safe and taken care of by locals in towns you've never dreamt of much less heard of? I have no Clue who does that.. apparently me!

So check mark.. Clueless #4

But being clueless is not entirely a **bad** thing. For myself I believe it's the times, in my life, that I have been the most certain, that I was right, (that I had a clue) That dammit I KNEW I was right!... it's been those moments where I have fallen the most firmly on my face and so there is peace and comfort in opening my mind, turning on what I call "the learning switch" and going into this with basically an empty head... ha ha ha...

That's easy for me, I am blonde after all (well at least after the bleach is applied I am)

Instead of an empty head, let's say an open heart and the inquisitiveness of a child. I am here to be taught and to have faith... To hopefully see that there is so much more beauty in the world, and in humanity, than I could have ever imagined.

This is why I come to the Camino to hopefully see some of the best of humanity. To lay down my misgivings about the world and instead be touched by whatever life has in store....

I believe the Camino has lessons for me and I am open to learning...(no pressure Spain)

Risk

As soon as we started talking with friends, family, clients, about our trip we started hearing the words..."You're so lucky". The word "Luck" is a huge pet peeve of mine... Luck is one thing I do not believe in.

My husband and I live a very, shall we say, ***different*** life. We have been happily married for over 20 years, no kids, self employed, travel extensively and well basically, in our opinion, we have a pretty kick ass life... and while this does not look like the average couple. Married (maybe not so happily), works 40+ hrs a week, kids, stressed to the hilt, on multiple medications, 1 week of vacation a year.

Our circumstances have nothing to do with luck and everything to do with... decisions and risks... we have taken.

I'll use our marriage as an example... My mother (love you mom) likes to say "you're so lucky you have Tony" as if somehow my life is that of a fairy princess because I found my prince charming. Well he is my prince charming and we do have the kind of relationship that I dreamed might be possible as a child (I say "dreamed" because I certainly wasn't seeing an example of it in my parent's relationship) but marrying Tony had nothing to do with ***luck***.

I made a huge decision...

I was not the kind of girl who dreamed of wedding days, in fact, I wasn't even sure I ever wanted to be married. But when I met Tony there was no doubt in my mind I loved him and would be with him the rest of my life. Then came the hard part I had to drop my single life, deal with a mother who was furious, at me, for getting married, so young, and ***risk*** everything to follow my heart and gut, move away and GOD FORBID marry a man ten years my senior.

No I don't believe in luck...

We're not *lucky* because we choose to work for ourselves... We took every risk involved and scrapped our way to where we are now.

We're not *lucky* because we don't have the stress of having children... we decided not to

We're not *lucky* because we travel around the country in a motor home... we sold everything and made it happen, taking every bump, bruise and joy that came with that decision.

We're not *lucky* we have our health. We have taken painstaking measures to educate ourselves, Taking the risk of regularly going against the establishment, learning what eating healthy means for us and understanding the profound importance of movement to the human body.

This rant leads me to here: We're not (as I've heard many people say) "lucky to be doing the Camino" We are taking all the risk and scrapping it together and making it happen.

I think many people don't follow their dreams because they have the misconception that some people are just *luckier* than them... and that's sad.

Maybe if the word "Luck" didn't exist and everyone clearly understood what it takes to make things happen; the decisions, choices and risks that must be made, people would live fuller lives.

<u>I wish I had been told this as a child: "There is no such thing as luck</u>... there is clarity of mind, focus and heart and then you apply a little bit of bravery, lean into your fear, take action, be disciplined, stay focused, be willing to

get really uncomfortable and you'll get there." It would have saved me a lot of time spent wishing.

In Brierley's book, *A Pilgrim's Guide to the Camino de Santiago*, he has a poem by **William Ward** that I think sums it all up beautifully:

To laugh is to risk appearing a fool
To weep is to risk being called sentimental
To reach out to another is to risk involvement
To expose feelings is to risk exposing your true self
To place your ideas and dreams before a crowd is to risk their loss
To love is to risk not being loved in return
To live is to risk dying
To try is to risk failure.
But risks must be taken
Because the greatest hazard in life is to risk nothing.
The people who risk nothing may avoid suffering and sorrow,
But they cannot learn, feel, change, grow or really live.
Chained by their servitude they are slaves who have forfeited all freedom.
Only a person who risks is truly free.

Signs

I think it's a girl thing but I LOVE signs... You know those moments of synchronicity when something so out of the blue happens you feel like the powers that be are shining a neon lit arrow in the direction your "supposed" to go. I regularly pray for these signs and I say "make it stupid easy Universe... I'm pretty thick. I need it stupid easy!"

Well we had one of those moments this weekend, Tony and I were hiking and training in the mountains of the Los Padres National Forest near Santa Barbara, California. After one of our hikes we drove to a little town called Santa Ynez for dinner.

Santa Ynez is a tiny town that borders, Buelton and Solvang. This area seems is the Southern most border of where the real "wine country" of California begins. Anyway we had never been to Santa Ynez but I felt drawn to see what the little town had to offer.

We had a disappointing dinner at an overpriced Mexican restaurant (there's nothing that irritates me more than paying too much for food you could get anywhere else at half the price and I love Mexican food so that really irks me) anyway walking back to our car Tony happened to walk up to a community bulletin board. You know the type where you may find lost dog photos or apartments for rent, etc.

So for no reason, other than we had parked directly in front the sign, he walks over and starts looking at what's posted. Then he laughs and yells over to me "Come here you've gotta see this". Figuring it's some kind of amazing deal on a house or something I walk over and scan the board. I'm squinting and trying to read the fine print on a house, for rent, and he says "No look closer" I strain harder and he says "No, you're missing it".

I step back realizing I'm not seeing whatever it is he's referring to and then I see it...

Smack dab in the middle of the board.

The biggest flier there... A seminar for The Camino de Santiago to be held at a local church September 6th!

Mind you this is April 10th...! Here is a flyer in the middle of nowhere, in a town we had no reason to go to, in a parking spot we had no reason to park in, on a board we had no reason to read, 5 months before the event was to be held. A sign that The Camino is the correct path for us.

All I could think is the probability of seeing this sign has got to be mathematically impossible... but God is not impossible!

Thank you for the sign... Keep em' coming!

To do lists SUCK!

In the days leading up to our trip I'm learning traveling out of the country for a month+ is hard to organize!

From setting up automatic bill pay, to paying bills in advance that can't be scheduled, this is a pain in the butt!

I feel like every time I cross something off the "to do" list I add 5 more things to it.

- Pay the vehicle registration (yes of course tags are expiring the day we come home)...
- Get adapters for all electric devices (cell phones, Ipad)... Forward all emails to an account we can access from anywhere...
- back up and figure out how to get access to all our websites, computer stuff, etc. ...
- buy all hiking stuff (shoes, back pack)...
- return everything that doesn't work, or fit, re-buy and try again...
- figure out what the HELL we're going to do with the dogs...
- figure out where to store motor home (aka our house. Yes we currently live in an RV more on that later)...
- Put everything in order to keep our business running while we're gone (Thank God for an amazing staff)... Pack...
- Train... and of course do all the daily tasks you normally do.

AGGGGHHHH!

Let's just say waking up in night terrors from lists of things to do is becoming a normal occurrence. During the day I meditate on it, relax, force myself to "See it as Perfect" and focus on the outcome I want and it all makes sense.

At night though after all my calming techniques have been exhausted I sometimes have to "pull out the BIG GUNS"

So I turn on Cheers... "Where everybody knows your name and their always glad you came" Ahhhhhh.....

Thank God for the mind numbing effects of television. It speaks to that out of control corner of my brain, shuts it UP, and peace reigns.

Let it Go

Typically on a vacation, or trip of any kind, (or average day for that matter) I have everything planned out well in advance. Excursions booked, meals planned, of course reservations made (months in advance).

Our journey on the Camino, however, will be the opposite of that... For approximately 34 days we will be "winging it"... or at least I'll be doing my best to get over the habit of pre-planning, planning, and then second guessing my planning. Because one way (the most common way) to approach the Camino is simply to take your guide book and walk to the next village or town that you think you can make it to and "have faith that the Camino will take care of you".

Most people average about 15 miles (24k) a day but there are so many villages, along the way, you can easily make it shorter, or a longer day, at any given time.

Because of this people generally do not book their rooms in advance and except for hiring a company to plan out your entire trip and book all your rooms in advance (last I checked at about $3400 per person) you CAN'T book rooms in advance... you simply walk and when you get to the next village you find the albergue (what we in the States would call a hostel) and see if they have beds available.

Most of the time they do, you pay and go pick a bunk, reserving it by unceremoniously throwing your sleeping bag on top of the bunk.

Tony is very comfortable with this and feels the Camino will take care of us...

I on the other hand am pretty uncomfortable with this style of travel. This for a Type A planning person, like me, is a night mare!

And if left to my own devices would cause me to spend every moment of my 6-7 hour walk worrying about whether we would get a bed for the night or not.

Here is where the life lessons began...

"Shut Up Molli, have faith, it will all work out."

Picture the outcome you want, clearly in your mind, focus for a moment and then LET IT GO! I knew this was my choice. Your other option is to worry yourself sick and have a horrible trip because this scenario is going to happen every day for the next 34 days.

This is how the mind works, if you let the portion of your mind designated for worry (I call it the "nut") take over it will happily drive you mad and run the show.

You are the boss and you are 100% in control of your thoughts. This is one of the most important lessons I have learned in my life and this trip has already been a test of utilizing this tool.

Shut up and let it go... A quiet mind is a far more useful tool than a worried one. It's in peace that we find our answers not in stress.

The solution to the problem does not exist at the same level of consciousness as the problem.

More Signs

As I mentioned I love signs!!! Those moments of synchronicity when it seems like your Guardian Angels are sending you a neon lit arrow pointing the way towards your ideal path... (Those kind of Signs...)

Well we had another one... I had been STRESSING OUT (shocking I know!) over what we were going to do with our dogs. I knew my sister Rose was happy to take care of them but of course it got complicated... Recently having broken up with her boyfriend, she was moving, smack dab in the middle of our trip and that meant the dogs

A. wouldn't know their new surroundings...
B. The place she was moving might not allow dogs...
C. She offered to stay in our motor home and "Rv/dog sit" but she works long hours and the dogs can't be left alone, for long periods of time, because they can't get outside to do their business!

Which led to us mulling it over and over and over...

We love our dogs like children. We have never left them for an extended period of time and this was killing us!

Then one night we went to a single A Baseball game (something we love to do) and standing in front of us, in line, to buy tickets, we see a guy with a bright green shirt on that read "George's Pet Sitting". I saw it and shrugged it off because "I'm not going to hire some random pet sitter"... (close minded much?)

So Tony elbows me and I nod... "yes I see it".... still ignoring (Remember I need those neon lit blinking arrows) and then...

George of George's Pet Sitting turns to us, out of everyone else in line, and says "do you need tickets?" And hands us a free ticket to the game!...BAM... there's my arrow.

I laughed and said "Thank you and you know what? We also need a pet sitter" and he said "Awesome a win- win" Since then we have met with him a couple times, in preparation, and each time he puts us more and more at ease and we find we have more and more in common.

His wife is an avid fitness enthusiast, runner, etc. and they treat their dogs very similar to us, regularly taking them hiking etc.

So there's no such thing as a coincidence...

Thank you Universe!

One major thing checked off the list! Rose will stay in the motor home, giving her more time to look for a place, the dogs will have the comfort of knowing their surroundings, and George gets a long time loyal client and will make sure the dogs are not locked up all day. This is what I prayed for a solution that worked out "for the highest and best good of all involved".

There's always a way we just have to be open enough to see the opportunities...(and the neon blinking arrows)

Ultreia on to the next challenge...

Physical changes to our body's

As the owners of a health and fitness company we're very in tune with our body's. We eat healthy, exercise regularly (of course)...

The schedule below is a typical day for us.

This schedule is about to be completely turned upside down on its head and for one of the first times, in our adult lives, we will have very little control over what we eat and when we eat... Which means...

I have no idea what's going to happen to my body!?!

A typical day for me looks something like this:

-**Wake up 4am** to teach our fitness boot camp (or if a non boot camp day sleep till 6am)
-Coffee /banana or date 3-4 mile dog walk
-**9:00**- green smoothie (lots and lots of greens, water, 2 bananas, 1 orange blended in a Vitamix blender)
- answer emails, write, coaching calls, etc.
-**10:30** Gallo pinto (black beans and rice with a fried egg and salsa on top)
- back to work
- **12:30** lunch typically a large salad
- work
- **2:00** workout (If I'm training for something specific whatever is on my schedule for that day otherwise, body weight strength training, joint rotations, hike, etc.)
- **after work out snack** turkey roll up (2 ozs of turkey breast with spinach rolled up inside) or more smoothie, celery and salsa
- **4pm** short dog walk
- answer any remaining emails
- **6:00** make dinner (when it comes to what we eat at home I'm a creature of habit typically a protein like Salmon, steamed vegetables and a salad, or home made

tacos, or Lentils with sauteed kale, something along those lines) lots of vegetables, lean proteins and very few processed carbohydrates.

But for the next several weeks all this is about to change RADICALLY!

The movement part is not a huge stretch for us... as I said "we move a lot!" but what will be entirely different is our food intake...

No green smoothies... no access to a kitchen (much less a Vitamix)... we won't even have control over what times of day we get to eat. In Spain it's the "norm" for restaurants and cafes to be closed from 2-4pm for "siesta" with dinner happening not until around 8:30pm.

8:30!!! If I'm walking 15+ miles a day I'm going to be in bed by 8:30 not eating dinner!!!

Suffice it to say life is going to be very different for the next several weeks... I figure I will lose weight because of not having access to our typical foods, I'll be starving! But then again, you never know, I may go berserk on salami, hard cheeses, wine, wine, wine, and what I've been told is some of the best bread in the world and I may even gain weight, even with all the activity (I can eat a lot ;-)

Whatever happens it will be quite the adventure and I intend to not hold back and experience all that Spain has to offer to the fullest (and share it with you here)

On a side note... I am not the least bit concerned over whether I gain or lose weight, only curious, because of course as soon as we get back it'll be right back into a normal, healthy, routine and whatever damage I have done will be quickly reversed... It's very empowering to *know* exactly how to change your body and it's something that we try to impart to all my clients.

Your body isn't happening to you. You can learn exactly how to transform it ,into what you desire. To visit our <u>health and fitness blog</u> check out our "normal" life here. Part of the adventure for me will be living a life so different than our daily routine.

We shall seeeeee........

On a mission to find the perfect shoes...

We've all been there (especially if you're training for an athletic event) the maddening search for the "perfect" shoes.

Do you go minimalist, extra cushion, or somewhere in between?

Light weight or Heavy and tough?

Waterproof or breathable?

Then even when you make these decisions and find the "perfect" shoe that doesn't mean it will fit... *you*... perfectly. It drives you crazy right?!

For the Camino your feet and your shoes become your #1 priority because there is no break. Every day you have to stuff your feet into the same shoes... no matter how beaten up, blistered, achy, or swollen they may be, your feet don't get a break. Making your prior training and breaking in of your shoes of the utmost importance!

You do pass through major cities so worst case scenario you can stop and buy a new pair of hiking shoes but what is the likelihood that after all your searching at home you're going to bop into a store and find the perfect shoe to relieve your pain? Not really something we want to test out.

So we've been obsessing even more than we normally do over shoes...

And my sweet husband has gone off the deep end...

Guess which of these 3 shoes he's thinking he's going to be able to walk 500 miles in?

Yep... the Sandals

Did you guess right? If you know us you probably did :-) you probably said "Let's see what's the most insane choice there?... Ahhh yes the sandals... that's Tony"

Okay in his defense, for years, we have been huge proponents of the minimalist shoe movement.

Your foot is meant to be barefoot, not clubbed into a heavy pair of shoes. The bottom of your foot actually gets feedback from the ground when you walk, stand, and run, and sends info to your brain letting the rest of your body know how to respond.

When you wear shoes your sending misinformation and it's kind of like your body is walking blind. Your senses don't fire on all cylinders and this often leads to trouble.

In addition to that shoes cause horrible walking and running form which leads to more cases of injury... If you're a runner and you ever have to stop running due to Hip pain, knee pain, ankle, shin splints this can all be rectified by correcting your running technique.

You can test this out for yourself, go for a jog with your shoes on and then take your shoes off and gently, carefully, run about 100 yards with no shoes. You will see instantly that your running form changed completely.

Most people, while wearing thick soled modern day shoes, run with a "heel strike" meaning your heel hits the ground initially, and sometimes quiet hard as you come down.

When you take off your shoes and run barefoot, you see that you immediately stop "heel striking" and you naturally take a shorter stride. Your foot comes down more towards the mid or ball of your foot. This is proper running form. Being a "heel striker" only happens because we wear thick soled shoes, making it too easy to be a "sloppy" runner and it is the leading most cause of injury in runners.

We aren't proponents of going entirely barefoot, however, because concrete, asphalt and modern day walking environments, are entirely different than what would have existed in nature. The best we can do in modern day is walk barefoot when your surroundings safely permit it, to strengthen your foot, and wear a moveable, breathable shoe without a thick sole (minimalist) so that your foot can get the information from the ground it's designed to.... (God made you pretty freakin' perfect and we keep F---'ing it up)

Tony has been wearing Vibram Five Fingers for years so he has taken the time to strengthen his foot assuring that his foot, and lower leg muscles, are healthy and strong enough to wear the sandals, I just worry about the elements, being cold, stubbing a toe, etc.

The sandals are Luna by Barefoot Ted... if you've ever read **Born to Run** you remember Barefoot Ted and his famous running sandals (and if you are at all interested in running or starting to run read the book...it's awesome!). Well Tony finally tracked them down and now 2 weeks before we leave he's trying to get his Luna sandals dialed in so that he can wear them on the Camino.

He plans to wear his Vibram Five Fingers with socks, in cold weather and his "Jesus Sandals" as we fondly refer to them whenever the weather is warm...

Wish us (and his toes) luck!

If loving you is Wrong…

We had our dogs, Seren and Jazz, in a hotel one night. It was about 11pm and I was walking down the hallway back to our room, after their last pee break for the night, and we passed a man, maybe in his 50's and an elderly woman, probably his mother, entering their room.

My dogs were actually being behaved (shocker) and we were quietly walking past them, when the man grumbled under his breath in a very thick, what I would guess was some kind of Russian or Eastern European accent, something to the effect of "There are people without homes or food and these people bring their animals into a hotel".

He said it with such seething venom, in his voice I couldn't help but be taken aback. His anger took my breath away and for a moment my stomach turned. We didn't engage him in any way, we just quietly kept walking to our room and he didn't engage me. The comment was made more to the woman, with him, definitely so that I would hear, but he wasn't addressing me directly just making sure I heard.

Of course it made me sad that someone would have so much anger and rage inside them they would need to launch their opinion, to a stranger, who was not harming anyone… but I completely see where he was coming from. I get the juxtaposition… Add to that it was late at night and they appeared to be just checking in.

He was probably exhausted and grumpier than usual but I can also imagine the things this man has seen in his life. I know that children go to bed hungry around the world, while my dogs get fed home cooked meals. I get that...

But I also know that being cruel to animals, or anything else for that matter, does not *fix* the problems of the World. Rage only begets more rage.

The love and compassion, I am fortunate enough, to be able to show my dogs helps me be more loving to humans... not less.

In fact it was my love and need to just get my dogs away from this man, that night, which caused me to quietly walk away instead of confronting him with my opinion (of course the comment wouldn't have been made because the dogs wouldn't have been there but you get my point). His rage and anger would have been there with or without the dogs, I'm sure he would have found something else to say.

I'm sharing this story with you so that you understand that I get I'm over the top when it comes to my dogs but instead of looking at it like I'm crazy, I invite you to look at it from this angle... when you feel love for something you spread more love. How is truly loving anything a problem? Love is unlimited it's not a finite resource.

When you love, you love more, you love deeper. When you hate, you hate more and you hate deeper. That man hated and he will continue to hate. I can see where he's coming from and I forgive him and wish him peace.

You never know what someone's story is until you ask them... Dogs, in a way, have taught me how to love.

Growing up my father was an animal trainer. When I was born he was an elephant trainer. Around that time my mom insisted he train something other than elephants for fear of my safety. She didn't want a little baby crawling around elephants and so he picked up where his father left off and took over a comedic dog act. (I guess that guy better watch out I could have been walking down the hall with an elephant ;-)

And so from the time I was born I had no less than 12 dogs around me, at all times. Literally dogs were my life. They were my best friends, my job, my livelihood. I protected them and they protected me. Dogs were one of the first things in my life I felt *real* love for.

I'm kind of like a "raised by wolves" kind of kid and quite frankly when I see an animal hurt it bothers me more than when I see a human hurt. I just see it as, the vast majority of the time a human has a choice in the matter and an animal does not.

Again I know that means there's probably something not connecting right in my brain but at least you know a little of my background now and might give me a little leeway for more weirdness. On the Camino I fear seeing any cruelty to animals.

I HATE (dammit there's that word) the concept of Bull fighting... and it is Spain's national past time. Encountering Bull fighting will be unavoidable. It's all over Spain and summer is the time of year when many of the festivals are going on.

I HATE seeing animals mistreated before they are killed to be eaten. I am not a vegetarian but I do not understand why we can't show them compassion and help them to live a happy, comfortable life, while they are alive.

I know that because of my deep hatred for these things I will be confronted with this on the Camino. The Camino helps us work out our issues and animal cruelty is a BIG issue of mine.

The only way to neutralize this is to feel love for the people around me, whether I agree or not. If I hate the people around me for what they do, I am the only one experiencing the poison.

If I verbally attack them they will feel threatened and defend... If I feel love... everything, including me, has an opportunity to change.

if I can't find a way to love... I am no different than the anger the man showed me in the hallway...

And then there were 3

A friend of ours set out this year to do the PCT...

The PCT (Pacific Crest Trail) is a trail that runs 2663 miles (4,285 km) from the border of Mexico up through California, Oregon and Washington to the border of Canada and it has become, shall we say, a hiker's pilgrimage to do the whole thing in one long "through" hike.

There are 3 long distance trails, I feel, you hear people talk about the most commonly the PCT, the AT (Appalachian trail) which is on the East coast of the US and runs from the state of Georgia up to Maine some 2,200 miles (3,500 km) and the Camino.

These trails could not have anything less in common so it drives me crazy when people bring them up in the same sentence.

The PCT runs through forests, mountains and deserts...

You pass through very little civilization. There are no (or very, very few) cafes, no hostels, no beds for the night...

Just you, your camp fire and a tent...everything you need on a day to day basis must be carried on your back. From camp stove to sleeping quarters to all your water and food because you may not see a town for days on end.

A whopping 1500 people a year complete the PCT and although you do run into plenty of fellow hikers you spend most of your days from the moment you crawl out of your tent in the morning to crawling back in it at night...
ALONE.

Sure there are campgrounds and meeting places along the way but when you consider that you'll be out there walking for 5 months straight a party here and there doesn't add up to much companionship.... If you take on the AT or the PCT be prepared for a lot of Nature a lot of camping and a lot of alone time.

The Camino on the other hand is a social event in comparison.

Over 200,000 people a year do at least some portion of the Camino. So not only are you seeing numerous Pilgrims everyday you are walking into villages with hotels, cafes, hostels, every night. There is not one night on the Camino where you have to use a tent (well unless you get lost). There are communal dinners, breakfasts, sleeping quarters (often sleeping 10 or more per room) and even communal showers!!!

You will not be alone for long on the Camino unless you make a concerted effort to do so.

So back to our friend, James, well about 19 days and 266 miles into his PCT adventure he decided that much solitude was not for him and came off the trail. Knowing he was in a unique situation and had scheduled out 5 months of his life to "through hike" the PCT the second he called us to say he had come off the trail, the first words out of my mouth were "are you going to do the Camino with us"?

This hike is made for him... No literally the Camino is also called "The Way of St. James"... Ha ha ha. He has to do it!

Well at that moment he said no (I think anything, at that moment, would have lost out to a hot bath and comfortable bed) so my timing may have been a little premature but 2 weeks later he was in!

He'll tell you I "talked him into it" but really all I did is talk about it and there was no stopping him...

Well once his husband, Brian, gave him his blessing that is. (Thanks for letting him go Bri... We wish you were coming too...)

So now there are 3 gringos and we're so HAPPY! James is like a brother to me, kind of like a twin brother, we think the same, so often it's eerie...

We have been on many adventures together Australia where all 4 of us climbed the Sydney Harbor Bridge. Amazing! The bottom of the Grand Canyon hiking to Havasupai falls...even more AMAZING! ... Mt. Whitney (in one day)...

We even have matching tattoos not because we got it together but because I stole it from him :-)... Trained for Ironmans... Half Dome in Yosemite...The list goes on and on.

Oh and we all met at a firewalking seminar. Where we were taking a course to learn to become Fire Walk instructors so that gives you a little bit of an idea of how much trouble we can all get in together!

Ultreia for three!

Living in an RV

About two years ago I came up with a crazy plan (yes another one), I convinced Tony we should sell everything move into an RV (more specifically a motor home) and travel around the U.S. documenting health and fitness success stories.

A. We had always wanted to live in an RV and travel around the country and
B. I thought it would be really cool to collect stories from people, in all walks of life, who had experienced inspiring weight loss and health success. I imagined a place, on line, where people could go and see hundreds of stories, follow a different story every day, and become addicted to watching them. Fascinated by the variety, viewers would gain momentum, and one day see someone they really resonated with and that would be their "tipping point" and thus become inspired to create a healthy success story of their own.

We called it *Change the W.A.V.E.* which stands for Change the Way America Views Exercise. We wanted to show that exercise can be fun and how many different things you can do to be healthy. There's not just one way there are many, many, ways. Find something you love and your life will change easily without effort. If you're forcing yourself to go to the gym or eat a salad it's never going to last.

Anyway.... Two years later our wave project had fizzled to little more than a puddle. I won't go into all the details here but suffice it to say I failed to realize, in order to make a nice looking video, you might have to have some video editing skills, and equipment. I still love the idea but we diverted our attention and so it's on the back burner.

Although we didn't take the Nation by storm with our project, Tony and I did completely change our own wave which sometimes I guess is the most you can ask for.

We did sell everything: 1 House, 1 car (kept one to tow), and contents of entire 3400 sq ft house. That was a journey... and we LOVED it!

Imagine opening up every cupboard and drawer in your house and taking everything out. Now you have to get rid of all of it because once you move into an RV you have no room to keep it! We weren't interested in putting everything in storage because we needed the money from the sale to fund the project and so it had to go. Yard sales, craigslist, ebay, you name it we used it.

I was surprised that the little stuff was pretty easy to sell it was the big things; couches, entertainment centers that were hard but we did it. Weeks and weeks of emptying cupboards... the stuff just seemed to multiply.... whittling it down to the bare essentials seemed an insurmountable task at times.

Emotionally it was only a little stressful, not so bad, there were only a few items that were hard to get rid of but you know what's funny? Even the things I really thought I'd miss... the ones that were tough to let go of... Once they were gone I never looked back. I didn't end up missing them even for a second. It was really weird!

We had become minimalists and we had done it in about 2 months time! And we were finding we LOVED IT!

Talk about riding a wave right?

This new lifestyle we have grown accustomed to prepares me, I think, in some odd ways for the Camino.

I used to be a little obsessive about cleanliness. I was the type that would wash the dishes before putting them in the dishwasher. Tony would say "If you're going to wash them why are you bothering to put them in the dishwasher?" and I would say "to sanitize them ;-)".

I would bleach and sanitize our washing machine with a pure white load of clothes and then rewash them before moving on to the rest of the colored loads... my washing machine was meticulous. I once spent from 3am to 3pm, on my hands and knees, cleaning the grout of our 12 inch tile floor, with a tooth brush, because it looked so pretty.

If my neighbors could have seen me they would have thought they were living next to a meth head. But no I just love cleaning... but I also thought I "needed" things to be just so in order to be Okay. I was uneasy when I saw dirt and that meant I was letting things outside of me determine my happiness. Not cool... The dirt was renting space in my head.

So all that OCD behavior had to go when we moved into "Rexi" (as we lovingly refer to our motorhome).

Now -I have to use a Laundromat now and unless you want to go bankrupt, on quarters, you do not get the opportunity to pre wash or clean the machines in any way. You just throw your loads in and wham bam thank you mam that's what you get. Not only are the machines not spotless, by any means, you are washing your clothes after hundreds and hundreds of strangers!

It's awesome because you realize how much B.S. you were holding on to. I had to get over germs and fast! I would say "can I let that story go?" and answer back "yes!" and move on.

After all how you view the world, the definition you give it, is all just a story in your head and you have complete control over that story. It's your story and you can let it go and write a new one.

Tony loves laundromats now... He loves that instead of the wash being an all day affair you get to throw 4 or 5 loads in at once and an hour and half later... they're all done (That part is pretty cool).

Now- I wash dishes by hand... yep by hand and sometimes with very little water. If your motor home is parked somewhere where you are not "hooked up" meaning the only water you have access to is the water in your RV's holding tanks than you have to conserve and that means learning to wash your dishes very differently, wet, turn off water, soap, scrub and then rinse quickly. I crack up thinking how different this is from what I used to do. God was I a water waster! Living in California that's no joke these days. I feel awful but boy do we make up for it now.

These things have prepared me for the Camino in unexpected ways. When we get the opportunity to wash our clothes on the Camino... guess where it will be? Not in my own personal washing tub, I'll tell you that much. It will be in machines that have been used by pilgrims, just as sweaty and dirty as we will be... Woo hoo thanks to my Rexi training I will not have a panic attack the first time I see the laundry facilities.

Showers will be short and sweet, even if you do get hot water, you have to conserve so the next pilgrim has some. Water on, wet yourself, water off, soap up, water back on to rinse... 2- 5 minute showers max...voilà!

From a house to a motor home... now a motor home to just a pack on our backs. For 30+ days we will live with no more than about 20 possessions each.

This should be interesting. I feel the wave building again and I'm ready to ride it in baby!

A Dream

I had the coolest dream last night. It seemed like a very short dream and it happened right before I woke up but it was powerful... In the dream I was with a tall figure, I think it was male but that's just the impression I got. I can't remember what the figure looked like. He treated me with respect as if we were equals but he was teaching or showing me something about the way I walked.

It was like we were communicating many things through our movements. I was walking very quickly, and pointedly, as if I were "on a mission" somewhere "very important, very urgent" and he seemed to agree but showed me if I slowed down a bit what that would mean.

I had more authority. When I slowed down... I could feel the shift.

Then he had me take it down another gear and I could sense a difference again and how effective the change was.

We did this, three or four times, until he showed me how to stroll with my arms behind my back. The way you would if you were contemplatively walking around a garden, chatting with a colleague or philosophizing about the cosmos.

It was a powerful dream because I could feel the point of it.... SLOW DOWN. (Ha ha haha insert neon blinking arrow here :-)

I have been on such a mission. I'm so tired from all that has gone into putting this trip together. I have been barreling full steam ahead and now whoever this was, in my dream, just told me it's time to slow down and appreciate the subtleties of the moment and how much more there is to be gained and shared this way.

That will be a tough lesson for me to implement but I will do my best.

Thank you whoever you were...

Spoiler Alert I did not heed the advice in and I paid for it!

Our first day in Paris

I am on zero sleep right now... went to bed at 12 and woke up wide eyed and bushy tailed at 2:30 so I apologize in advance for this rambling, delirious post... but here goes... our first day in Paris!

From the beginning... The flight over was uneventful... Ten hours on a plane just sucks no matter how you cut it. Every time I get off a long distance flight I swear it will be the last time I go without being able to afford first class, just because I WANT TO LAY DOWN SO BADLY ! It just sucks to sit up when all you want to do is lay down and sleep.

Other than that it was all good... The flight attendants came around with drinks and I asked if I could order a bloody Mary (I was trying to have a little kicker to help send me off to La la land) and she said "absolutely" and asked if she took cash or only credit and she said "drinks are complimentary"... What? Awesome!

Then when they brought dinner around asked if we would like wine with that and again I'm like "Ummm Yeah!" and she hands me, a very large, single serving bottle of red wine from Spain and it was De-lish! Insert happy dance here... It still didn't put me to sleep though :-(

Combined I think we each slept about 4 hours on and off. When I couldn't take it anymore I curled up into a little ball on my seat and Tony let me lay across his lap for two solid hours (this was my only shot at sleeping) and his poor legs went to sleep but he wouldn't wake me... what a sweetheart!

All in all flight was great. We get to London's Heathrow Airport and have some ridiculousness at security where they're basically checking everybody's everything and it takes us about an hour to get out of security but we figured it was "entertainment" for us... What else would we be doing but sitting at the gate? Might as well sit at security and watch people freak out about being searched... ha ha.

So walking through Heathrow, looking at the shops I see a cute little dress and this is when it hits me... Shit! We're in London and I'm about to be in Paris and I CAN'T SHOP!!! I literally can't take anything else in my backpack on the Camino... This includes souvenirs and I immediately started seeing things that were "perfect" for each of our friends... Ughh! Ok new battle plan if there's something someone "couldn't live without" I could have it shipped. In the meantime I'll just take pictures of what I would have bought them and hope that suffices.

Then we had to get from London to Paris.. Flight to Paris, uneventful (which is a very good thing... you never want an "eventful" flight :-). We once flew into Denver and it was so "eventful" we both almost pooped our pants (if you get my drift)... and if Tony gets nervous on a flight then I know it's something to worry about... Tony does not get nervous.

We land and breeze through Customs because all we have is our itty bitty back packs, that's nice. and head out to the street to find a cab. We start pinching ourselves... "We're here... we're really here!!!"

Our taxi driver is an absolute doll. A man probably in his early 60's, I didn't catch his name. Immediately I can tell he is very proud of his city. Not in a arrogant way but in a very genuine, quiet way. He mentions that he has traveled to D.C., New York, Atlanta, San Francisco and a few other U.S. spots and I can tell by what he doesn't say that he prefers Paris.

I start looking around while we're chatting and you can feel and see the vibrancy of the city immediately. Bustling and hectic but in a positive, energetic way.

We tell him about the Camino and it turns out he owns a home in Spain so he's very familiar and very excited for us and our "grand adventure". He drops us off and already it's like we're saying goodbye to a friend he shakes our hands and wishes us well. I don't remember his name but I wish I had caught it... very sweet man...

Our friend, James, has agreed to meet us at our hotel (he's staying at another hotel a little bit down the road) but he's there to greet us, at ours, when we pull up. We check in... Super sweet girl at the front desk, we run upstairs and literally throw our packs down and head out the door.

Our mission to see as much of Paris in the next 6, or so, hours as possible. Since James arrived a few days earlier I asked him to please show us around and he was totally up for it. He had our itinerary set and we hit the subway headed towards Notre Dame... and then we got trapped in the subway... Just for a moment (and completely because of our own bone head move).

We threw our passes away, as soon as we went through the first gate, thinking we wouldn't need them again. Well we did and we couldn't get through the 2nd gate and onto our train. We tried to retrace our steps back to the trash can, we had thrown them in, but we got lost and so for about 10 minutes we were just circling under the streets of Paris like rats in a maze. It was hysterical! I'm like "I'm in Paris and I can't see a damn thing because I'm under the freaking ground!". We had to exit, buy new tickets and start all over... DUH! But then we were off! Notre Dame here we come!

He planned to have us take the subway to Notre Dame and then walk along the Saines back towards The Louvre. On the way we were hungry so Tony and I got a little nippy at each other because we waited too long to eat... It was one of those you're so excited to eat your first food in Paris you won't make a decision kind of moments. I finally saw an alley way and I remembered so many of our friends saying "just find an alley and get lost down it and you'll find the most amazing surprises"... so I turned us down an alley and right there, just as promised, it was like we had stepped into another secret world. All these beautiful shops and restaurants tucked away. So cool!

I finally went with the first baguette sandwich I saw, Jamon and chèvre. Tony an almond croissant... very tasty. We ate as we walked and perked right back up and then we got to the Louvre... From here I'm just going to say this place is freaking AMAZING and I don't just mean the Louvre I mean the entire city. I never expected to be this impressed.

We were speed/ marathon sight seeing Paris though so we had to make up all the "history" on our own... "Gringo style"... We cracked ourselves up making up stories about the significance of all the statues, monuments, etc.

We had a blast but it's definitely not how I would recommend you do Paris. After seeing the city myself now I understand why my friends, who had visited Paris, all looked at me like I was on crack when I said we were only going to have about six hours there... It would take weeks to properly see this beautiful city.

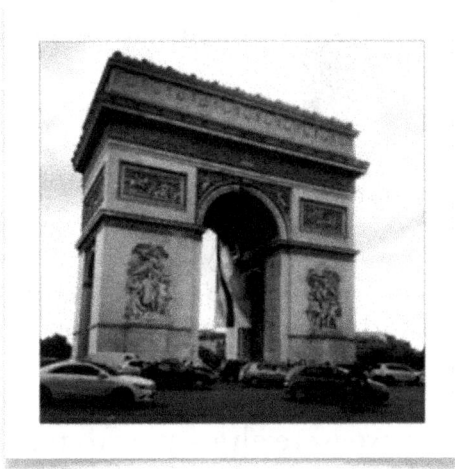

We packed as much as we could in... Thanks James for making that possible!
Walked from literally 4pm to 11pm only stopping for 1 espresso break and dinner (Steak and pomme frites) then to bed at midnight only to be as I mentioned in the beginning WIDE AWAKE at 2:30a.m. wish me luck sleeping tonight... Tomorrow is the Pyrenees... we're gonna need it!

More to follow when I can think (and get WiFi) again :-)

St. Jean Pied de Port

The most popular route for walking the Camino is the Camino Frances which begins in the town of St Jean Pied de Port. This is where we spent our first night.

We made our way from Paris to St. Jean today via a train through Bayonne and Biarritz. I say a "train" but what we actually did was purchase train tickets and were promptly put on buses. Which is fine, they were clean and comfortable.

In the bus/train station we were already surrounded by fellow peregrinos and began to make friends, instantly. We met a young man named, Adam, who had us in stitches from the moment we met him. Instant bond! A wonderful mother and daughter team from Napa, California. A solo man from Japan who didn't speak a lick of French, English or Spanish. Yikes, he's going to have an interesting trip! We did some charades for him to help explain that "yes, in fact, he was on the right track". I'm sure he was completely confused by the whole bus, train thing as well! And various other couples, primarily husband and wife teams. We all loaded up on two buses and made the breathtakingly, beautiful drive into St. Jean.

St. Jean is idyllic from the storefronts, to the cobblestone streets, to the natural environment, surrounding the place. It's straight out of a storybook!

Our hostel (albergue) for the evening is Gite Ultreia. We have a private room so we have yet to experience the "true" pilgrim adventure yet ;-) A sign hung on the door reads "Complet" (meaning no vacancies. This is what you don't want to see when you pull in to town! Luckily we had secured our room in advance but as we head out on the Camino we have no further reservations so it's all up to what the Universe has in store!

The stores here are adorable! I had to actually tie my arms down, to my sides, to avoid buying loads of souvenirs from the wonderful stores, in St. Jean. But alas that is not why we're here.

We're here to follow these symbols for the next 500 miles....and walk the Camino De Santiago.

This is the first arrow we saw. I hope they're easier to see than this one!

Okay that's all for now... It's 4:30am. alarm is set to go off at 5:30 for our first walking day...

Yikes Let the Camino begin!

Day 1... Finally! St Jean to Roncesvalles From Bonjour to Hola

The only way to describe today is AMAZING... I am speechless.

The first section of the Camino is notorious for being one of the most difficult parts. The first portion, out of St Jean, crosses over the Pyrenees mountains. If you remember in the movie *The Way* this is the spot where his son dies.

I always thought it was odd they would portray someone dying so close to having begun the journey but now that I have seen it with my own eyes, it's no longer a mystery why they wrote the story that way.

This area in bad weather would be treacherous! It's very steep and the weather can turn on you quickly. We were told today would be "sunny", by the visitor center, but I had a feeling it wouldn't be and it wasn't.

In the beginning of our hike we were socked in with such a thick fog that we were soaking wet within minutes of leaving our albergue. We were prepared though, with rain ponchos, and the nice thing was it kept us cool.

I have heard it said the Camino breaks into 3 portions; The first is life... the second death... and the third rebirth. As we started up the climb It felt more like the "death" part was starting... ha ha ha.

No I actually thought "this *is* exactly like life". I couldn't see anything but I knew there was so much more there. It was hidden and I had to have faith. I kept trying to prevent the elements from effecting me. As I put more protection around me I withdrew more inside myself. I realized that withdrawing from the world does not protect you. In the beginning to "protect" myself I put the poncho on... then I pulled the hood over my head. At this point my vision was obscured.

I couldn't see as well and I could no longer hear very well. As I "protected myself from the world" I realized I was no longer experiencing and I really wasn't any more comfortable then when I just took the hood down and let myself get soaked.

For me it was an analogy for life... when we try to protect ourselves we withdraw further and further from things that weren't going to hurt us in the first place.

During the hardest part of the hike (the beginning)

My initial thoughts were "this hike is no joke"... then we would turn the next corner and see an even steeper incline and I would say "this is NO joke" and then we would turn another corner and see more up and I said "Is this an F'ing joke?"

So I think you get the idea, there was a fair bit of up. Our first break came in Orisson where I had a $5 glass of fresh squeezed orange juice (THAT WAS TOTALLY WORTH IT!)

After Orisson the path let up a little. Don't get me wrong it was still up just no longer straight up.

My only disappointment for the day is the fog. We were socked in for the first half which meant we missed spectacular views.

I can't even fathom what we missed but the mist kept us cool and was magical in it's own way.

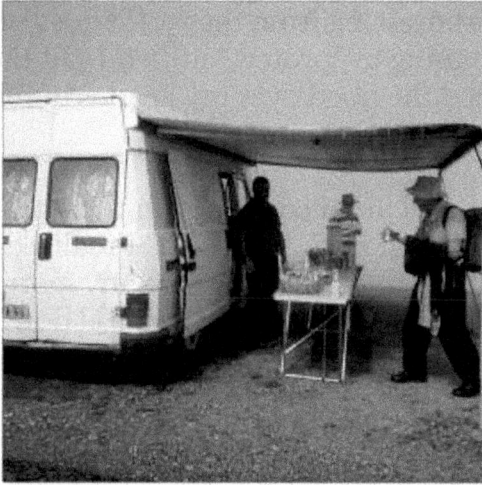

About half way there was a man with a "food van" on the side of the road. He had hard boiled eggs, fresh cheese, drinks. I had a hardboiled egg and it was just what I needed! Simple pleasures, YUM!

We kept climbing through the most beautiful valleys of green I've ever seen with animals walking right across the path and right up to us. *side note to all you crazy animal lovers out there (like me) you'll be happy to know every animal I have seen so far has looked like the happiest animal ever* And now I know why ranchers put bells around the necks of their livestock because you can't see them in the fog...but you can hear them!

And when the fog did finally break... It was Spectacular! Basically if you enjoy hiking, YOU NEED TO GET HERE! Not necessarily to do the whole Camino but visit the South of France and hike the portion from St Jean Pied de Port over the Pyrenees. The beauty is unprecedented.

There's a song by a woman named Oleta Adams that keeps running through my mind "*I don't care how you get here just get here if you can*".

We survived our first day on the Camino!!! We are thrilled with it and ourselves. So far it's been even better than anticipated... by a lot!

So far it's been even better than anticipated... by a lot! To top it all off we even had good food... We ate lunch at a Michelin rated restaurant in Roncesvalles "La Posas". The food was freaking amazing I have never had asparagus anything like this.

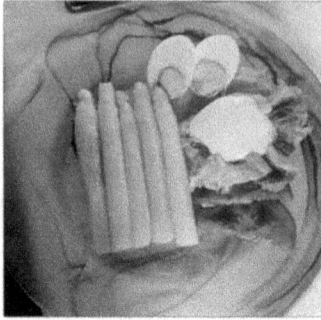

Oh and then there was dessert... The ice cream was out of this world... It was James' but I had a bite it tasted like strawberry and roses...

and Tony had the coolest dessert it was called "fruit topping" and we didn't know what it would be but when it came out it was such a treat because this is something he makes at home and loves. We call it "fruit cereal" just chop up a bunch of your favorite fruit and pour apple juice over it. We really thought Tony had made this up but here it was for him on the Camino...

Hmmm I think that was a little Camino gift for him.

Tomorrow is 12 miles (19km) downhill to Zubiri... woo hoo!!!!!

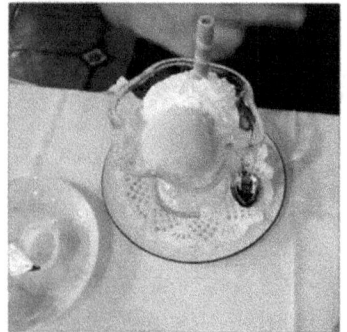

Our first "official" Albergue

I keep pinching myself... Did I die yesterday and is this heaven? Every second just keeps getting better... literally moment by moment it gets better to the point where we look at each other laugh and say "can it get any better?" because we can't imagine anything better, happening, and then it does... Weird!

This is last night's albergue in Roncesvalles Very well put together. It sleeps probably 200+ very comfortably... separate women's shower and men's, about 4 people per bunk area.

The albergue offers vending machines. As well as a large commercial kitchen where you can wash plates, get water, etc.

And guess what? They even had a laundry service! For 3.7 Euro the "hospitaleros" washed and dried a load of clothes for you. The place is brand new and very clean! When you're inside the albergue, you feel a bit like you're in a factory.

Step outside, though, and you are in a wonderful, tiny, hamlet with a beautiful church, large yard and a couple restaurants. With Wifi :-)

Oh and I call this the "scary, scary room" because they make you take off all your hiking shoes before you enter the albergue. Making this room one of the worst smelling things you'll ever experience.

While yesterday's lunch was amazing... last night's dinner, on the other hand, <u>was not</u>. It was our first "pilgrims meal" and well let's just say you knew why it was cheap. The choice was fish or pork and french fries and it made the worst banquet meal, you've ever had, look like a feast... But who cares it came with a bottle of wine and we were still full from lunch.

Ultreia onto Zubiri!

P.s. remember to visit our Blog www.PairofGringos.com because we have so many more pictures there we don't want you to miss out!

Day 2 I keep pinching myself...
Roncesvalles to Zubiri

We headed out this morning at 6:15 and those of you who know me are going to love this story...

We have a new friend Adam, and he said he wanted to try and walk with us today so we said "great meet us at 6:15".

Well 6:15 came and no Adam. If you know us you know what happened next....

Out the door we trotted, and actually I have to defend myself here because James was the one that was adamant we didn't wait a second longer (it wasn't just me this time) and so no Adam. Sorry dude that's just how we roll, don't take it personally!

So the three amigos headed out (sans Adam) headed towards Zubiri. It was 13 miles (21km) and promised to be downhill and nothing like strenuous hike we experienced yesterday. We were very much looking forward to an "easy" walk today and that's what we got! Yay!

We passed through beautiful farm land and had a slow decent into Zubiri with just a couple tiny up hill climbs. As we approached Zubiri I had spoken with several pilgrims along the way and everyone I talked with had decided to skip Zubiri and push ahead to a village 3 miles (5km) further down the Camino. Their reasoning being they wanted a shorter walk, the following day, into Pamplona so they would have more time there.

I passed this info on to Tony and James and we were debating it. When we got into town James said he wanted to sit down and rest his feet and we were all still debating what to do. It was still very early, 12:00, and it's in our nature to just keep pushing on but we torn because it was so beautiful, where we were, in Zubiri.

Then I took off my shoe to look at my right, pinky, toe which had been hurting since yesterday and gasped when I saw this.... A blister the size of the toe itself. Well that was my neon blinking arrow. I got the message (finally) it was time to stop, where we originally intended, and not push on.

Because of that decision we ended up having the most beautiful afternoon (seriously I can't imagine having a better time than we had today).

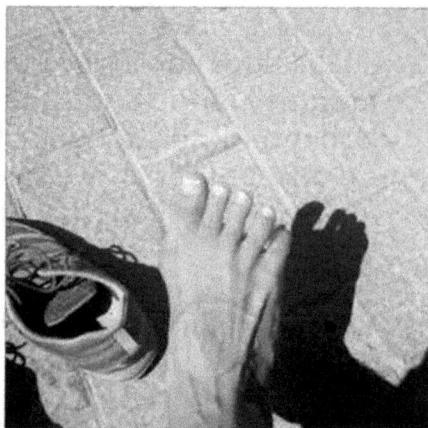

We had Paella, we grabbed a beer, we booked our room, in the most beautiful semi private (4 per room) albergue, Rio

Arga, for only 15 euro for the night which includes breakfast. They have a washer and dryer so we will have clean hiking clothes again tomorrow. They have a beautiful, clean shower with hot water and we're bunking with a fascinating guy, William, who has walked the Camino from Ireland making this his sixth week (cool right?)

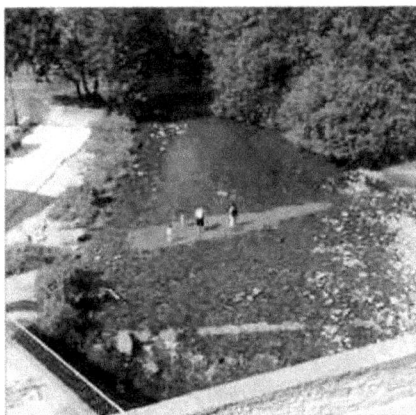

After lunch we headed down to the creek directly below our albergue.

On the Camino today I had said "wow it would be great to have a cold stream for my feet" and guess what showed up. The crazy thing is because of my incessant need to "just keep going"

I almost didn't stop here... Ridiculous!

This was my Camino lesson today. Do not follow the masses. Everyone had an agenda to go further and sacrifice today for tomorrow and so I almost did what they were doing instead of just enjoying the beauty I had right in front of me

So we had an amazing day soaking in the cold stream making lots of new friends. Adam even ended up catching up to us. He was in a lot of pain but he made it! We sat by the river for hours laughing our heads off and then everyone couldn't resist getting all the way in and swimming. Sorry no pic of that because we couldn't get the camera wet and besides one of the girls ended up getting naked (not me) so it's good we didn't get any x rated pics :-)

I've never seen that before. A woman just up and get completely naked in front of a group of strangers, in broad daylight, and go swimming, interesting.

I'm guessing 20% body fat percentage... Ha ha ha (you have to know me to get that one!)

Tomorrow is Pamplona... How much better can it get?

Lessons I took away from the Camino... Be here now

I can see now, very clearly, we are too distracted in our daily lives. The Camino takes away those distractions. When in life do we put down the phone, turn off the music, shut off the Television. Quit making "to-do" lists, in our minds? Stop asking ourselves "what's next?"

Never...

In the past couple years I had made a conscious effort to set time aside for meditation. In addition to that time my husband and I walk our dogs, in nature, every single day of the year without fail. These were the only moments we would spend purposefully "quiet".

Otherwise it was go... go .... Go.   What's next, next, next? We were rarely here, now, in the present moment. It's in this moment we quiet down enough to connect with God.

Even the small amount of time, we had been spending, had helped us become more peaceful, happier, people. But on the Camino you have time. Time to do nothing but be.

Even on the Camino it takes conscious effort to achieve this state. We started checking ourselves all day by repeating "Be here now" and we were seldom there... It took practice.

Walking the Camino in our every day lives... I don't believe it's necessarily this spot, on the planet, which creates the connection. It's the set of circumstances created here that are hard to recreate in your every day environment.

Step away from the world with all of its distractions for as long as you can. Start with 5 minutes, if that's all you've got, set a timer. If you can spare more time walk around the block for 30 minutes, without music, without anything and just be. As long as you keep saying "I don't have time" that's the story you will be telling yourself for the rest of your life. You are creating your story. If you don't like how it's turning out... tell yourself a new one. Try "How did I find this extra time so easily?" Asking yourself empowering questions gives your mind a puzzle it wants to work out.

Repeat to yourself "Be here now" and notice your surroundings. Notice how your mind was somewhere else... onto the next task... and bring it back to this moment. You are the boss. Your thoughts are not out of your control. Be here now and notice how the mind immediately quiets.

Since returning we are acutely aware of the myriad of distractions that come flooding back into our lives. It takes a much more concerted effort but it's still possible to be here now and quiet our minds.

I won't sugar coat this. Coming back was a dramatic difference. The distractions in our daily lives are completely out of control; Social media, texts, computers, televisions, traffic, to-do lists, it goes on and on. It was much harder to achieve the clarity of intention once we got back to the "real world"

And it took practice to initially disconnect when we got there. Some who read this, I'm sure, will say we never did.... but only we know the transformation that occurs within each of us. I know the level of consciousness I achieved, by quieting down, during that period of time is something I have never experienced before and my husband definitely experienced similar results (I know *this to be true because we are not the same people since returning home).*

But as I said it took a concerted effort to disconnect there as well. It doesn't just happen for you.

Meaning if you're clear and disciplined enough you can create the same thing from where you sit right now without traveling all the way to Spain.

Practice bringing your awareness back to the present, over and over again, throughout the day and stress will begin to dissipate. Be here now... It's the most important place you can be. Raise your energy where you are now and life can change.

Change is not coming because of something outside of you... You change here and now and the world around you has no choice but to shift.

Here (wherever that is, for you, at this moment) is a gift so
Take a deep breath and BE HERE NOW...

Day 3 Zubiri to Pamplona

Day 3 and we've already lost track of what day of the week it is. It seemed like Thursday but Tony was sure it was Friday, he was right (shocker). That's how much we have packed into two full days of walking. I have already completely lost track of time.

So far the routine has been leave at 6:30, walk about 15 miles (24km), get to the next village between noon and one, find somewhere to sleep for the night, shower, have lunch, walk around the village, drink a couple beers, struggle to get wifi (pronounced wee fee here), blog (pull my hair out because the weefee isn't working), have dinner and go to bed by 10.

Today the only change to this has been that instead of "walking" around the village (today's village being the beautiful city of Pamplona)... we're hobbling. Everybody's feet hurt!!! My pinky toe looks mighty grim. Dr. James (the "blister Doctor" the new nick name I gave him) has been closely attending my, rather large, blister.

See the problem is, as an athlete, I am very used to doing an event and being in pain... I can "push through" quite a bit. Here though is a different story because the Camino isn't one singular event, it's day after day, and James has more experience than either Tony or I on that subject.

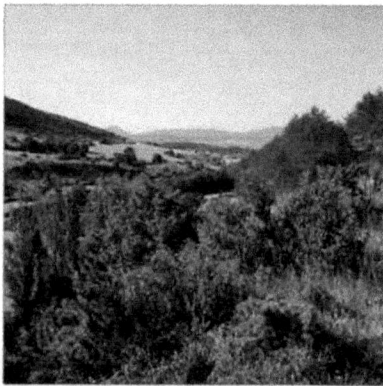

If i don't take care of my blister today, and let him wrap it up, then it might get to the point where I can't walk the next day... (But it's a story in my head and I can let it go).

Tony and James' feet are feeling the effects of having done a 50k at this point. They were doing good until we got into a city with hard pavement... everybody is just SORE but we're good!

Today the landscape changed from that of a forest to more farm lands and fields as we descended down into Pamplona from Zubiri.

Still absolutely beautiful but different. The weather also changed to more like we're used to at home, less humidity and about 85 degrees.

We passed another beautiful church with this bridge just outside. From our vantage point It looked like we were in a snow globe with all the pollen floating in the air.

This was our bunk mate from last night, William, from Ireland (he has been walking 6 weeks from Ireland) I walked a couple miles with him, this morning, as we entered Pamplona and he told us about a great Albergue in Pamplona, run by a German organization Freundeskreis Der Jakobuspilger, called Casa Paderborn.

He said it's known for being very good and they don't take reservations so it fills up quickly. I listened (neon blinking arrow) and we ended up rooming with Ursula or as we call her "dream girl". Ursula has blogged her dreams, every night, for the last 20 years and has completely transformed her life as a result. We felt honored to be able to spend time with her.

Walking into Pamplona the city's pavement felt hard and foreign to our tender feet which had become so accustomed to the dirt trails we have been walking on for the past several days.

After we were settled into our Albergue we headed out to discover Pamplona. We sat down at a restaurant (starving) and ordered two beautiful beers (1 for James, 1 for me, water for Tony) and food. The beers came, and before the food could get there who popped up but "dream girl" she asked to join us and we were thrilled to have her.

I had a wonderful talk with her. Another funny coincidence; when she sat down with us, she saw the beer I had ordered, completely by chance, and it ended up being the only beer she drinks, Leffe.

We had lunch and walked around Pamplona the 4 of us. We headed out to see the street the bulls run down (of course).

This is the building, and the square, where all the people stand before the bulls start running...

Kind of like the "start line" We took this picture during "siesta" about 4pm, when the streets were desolate, by 9:00pm the streets were packed!

While we were walking around we saw many butcher/meat shops and I wanted to taste some of the sausage.

I walked in and asked if I could buy one of the little "weenies" they look like a tiny little hot link, and the guy

was so nice he just threw open the lid of the canister and told me to take 1. How cool is that?!

Oh and that reminds me... The people in Spain have been fantastic!!!

Two people today yelled, from their cars, "Buen Camino" as they whizzed passed us. It's so fun to feel like you have the support of an entire Country behind you.

Tomorrow is another 15 miles (24km)... wish our feet well!

Day 4 Pamplona to Puente La Reina

Not to sound redundant but absolutely breathtaking! So far we love the Basque Country of Spain, amazing! We have entered into weather and territory that we're more familiar with. It was about 85 degrees Fahrenheit while we were walking today and I assume the mid afternoon got up to about 90.

We just spoke with our hospitalero/bar tender and he was explaining the difference / conflict between the Basque and Spanish regions, in this area, which goes back even before the Roman Empire, very interesting.

The Basque region has been amazing so I hope there are more similarities than differences. Their houses are amazing and immaculate, the people are friendly, the food is very good. The animals are very happy and well cared for.

We did 15 miles (24km) today and that's about our limit right now (I wouldn't want to do more). In a few days we'll probably be able to go a few more miles, a day, without issue but for now 15 hurts.

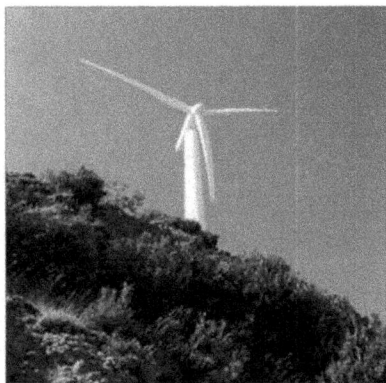

The climb out of Pamplona is breathtaking and of course the whole time you're anxiously anticipating the famous windmills and monument to the Pilgrims...

We climbed up through the windmills...

to a monument
for the Pilgrims

And down into the town of Puente La Reina. We couldn't
really decide on an albergue so we walked all the way
across town to the last one and checked in and then
promptly checked back out because we've been spoiled by
our last 2 accommodations.

Long story short... then James ran clear across back to the
start of the village (because he felt a little responsible for
not choosing the first nice one we saw. He had a sign and
failed to listen to it). He kindly booked our room while
Tony and I stopped and had lunch (I was famished). I had
an amazing goat cheese salad and Tony had his new "go
to" Atun which is tuna in Spanish, cute right?

This is the bridge out of Puente La Reina otherwise known
as the "Queens Bridge". The Queen had it built
specifically for the Pilgrims because it was difficult to
cross the river.

Our lesson for today... It seems that the Camino does not
understand "negatives". We say something like "Wow
there have not been any bugs" and all of a sudden we are
swarmed by bugs or "It would be wonderful to stick my

feet in a cold stream" and we have a cold stream beneath our hotel room.

Another example would be the second we say "I'm glad there are no steep grades right now" boom.... we're met by a steep incline within 5 minutes. Our thoughts seem to manifest very quickly here...

Just interesting to note. We're learning to be very clear with our intentions.

I may not blog tomorrow because it has been very difficult to get weefee... I may wait until we have a strong connection but now that I have said that the Camino will most likely provide a strong connection the rest of the way :-)

Lesson from the Camino... what you picture is what you get... See it As Perfect

This is a great lesson to be clear of thought and only focus on exactly what you want and not on what you don't want. The Universe does not understand negatives.

Whatever you are picturing, you're going to get more of...

When I say "there haven't been any bugs". What do you picture? Bugs right?

There is no such thing as a negative. You only get what you hold in mind... good or bad.

If you don't know what to picture just empty your thoughts completely... A quiet mind is far more useful than a busy one.

Begin to notice how much of your time is spent picturing what you don't want. The mind is only creative. What you spend your time thinking about makes a big difference in your life.

Practice on small things just bringing your awareness to this habit is half the battle. When you're struggling with something, even silly little things like opening a jar that's stuck. Stop for a moment and witness your thoughts... Are you picturing the struggle or are you picturing the jar being open?

Notice how much of your awareness and emotion is wrapped up in the drama of the jar not opening. Quiet your mind and hold an image of only what you want to have occur...

An open jar

and in that moment you will feel how much energy was going towards the opposite.

Analyze your thinking and correct it... It's the only way to gain, back, your true power.

Day 5 Puente La Reina to Estella

We were really "roughing it" last night. Here's a pic of last night's Hotel/ albergue
See perfect weefee today... I told you that's how it would go down.

Today we traveled 13.6 miles (22km) from Puente La Reina to Estella.

The pain is beginning to catch up with us. It waited this long to get us. Right now we're sitting on our respective beds, in a religious Albergue, known for its choir... (haven't heard them yet), asking each other to pass us things because our feet hurt so bad we refuse to put them down on the floor unless absolutely necessary.

Our energy levels and upper bodies are fine but our feet feel cobbled so James went on an ice bucket hunt and came back victorious. That was a great manifestation story. He was asking to borrow a bucket and they were reluctant to give us one but he pointed to one in a broom closet. It was dirty but he figured we would just clean it and use it. When he lifted it up and brand new bucket, which had been stuck to the bottom fell off, Voi la! Perfect bucket manifested, Nice!

We all tortured ourselves with 3 minute rounds in an ice water bath.

Others have been hurting for awhile but now we're right there with them. The sad part is when we pull into town we are in too much pain to walk around and see it, so a lot will be wasted on us, if we keep feeling like this.

We decided to start a bit later today because our hotel last night offered a buffet breakfast in the morning. Let me preface this by saying on The Camino "breakfast" consists of bread and jam/jelly/preserves and coffee... period.

That's it. It doesn't matter what they charge you or what they say... a Pilgrim's breakfast is= bread and jam. Tony doesn't want to see another piece of bread as long as he lives and I eat it just to sop up the caffeine I'm ingesting (plus the jam is really good).

So this morning the hotel promised a buffet breakfast and we were excited to have something other than bread to start our day. It was true and we had meats and eggs and orange juice and cheese and all sorts of yummy things so we ended up leaving at 8am instead of 6:30 as we have been.

It's very hot outside so that made today a little "extra special" considering we left a little later.

Leaving later meant we saw a new group of people. Think of it like the front of a race pack and the back. We have been with the front, today we got to meet the back. It's fun to be able to meet a new crop of people.

The landscape is much drier, now, and we are seeing a lot of what we think are oat, wheat, and poppy fields...

and big bushes of beautiful yellow flowers and lots of olive trees.

This is the view as we entered Cirauqui. A beautiful medieval town

We passed this local man, walking his dogs, as we entered into town. I love how they treat their animals here.

Almost always off leash but they carry one with them and when they come upon another dog, they quickly tie them up. When they pass humans they leave them off leash and the dogs completely ignore us... I LOVE it!

One of today's highlights was being able to walk into a church circa 1062 A.D. I 'm pretty certain that's the oldest building I've ever been in.

I pretended to remarry Tony here today, which ironically would be our first wedding inside a church (the first time was the Empire Mine in Grass Valley, Ca. Then we renewed our vows on a, deserted sand spit of an, island in the Caribbean. With the help of a sea Captain) and today in a church almost 1000 yrs old.

The graffiti on the trail, up until this point, has been basically non existent except for political statements and art. Here's Tony in front of a wizard sketch

They do a lot of amazing designs with their plants here..

We just happened by this. Mural of the continents sculpted out of plants.

Once we entered Estella there had just been a magnificent procession, through the streets. They were doing something with all these flower petals so I couldn't resist making a snow angel in them.

Yeah it's pretty magical...

Tomorrow is another "easy" day 13.6 miles (22km)... Ultreia!

Lesson from the Camino... Go at your own pace... It's not a race

As you walk along the Camino you run into the same people over and over... Sometimes this will seem very surprising to you because you will think you made different decisions and choices of places to stop and yet you'll still see the same people pop up... at least this is what happened to us.

Someone will appear to be much faster than you and you'll think "they'll be long gone soon" and then poof! There they are in the same town as you for the night.

The same goes for people who are much slower... One woman I nicknamed the "French Tortoise" because we were just like the fable of the tortoise and the hare. She was French and spoke no English so we never connected, verbally, but she stood out to me and we always waved and laughed when we passed each other.

She kept up her slow and steady pace and she looked like a tortoise because she had a huge back pack with a green rain cover, which she always kept over her pack. She also walked hunched over due to the weight of the pack making her appear even more like a turtle to me.

She left very early every morning and inevitably about an hour into the walk we'd pass her for the first time. Then we'd stop and eat and she would pass us and then we'd pass her again and usually see her later that night in the same town for the evening, only to start the whole race over again the next morning. I was so impressed by her slow and steady pace.

She was close to 70 and at the end of each day she ended up right where we were... I regretted not getting a picture of my "French tortoise". I looked back, one day, after leaving a café just outside of Burgos and I got the impression that was going to be the last time I would see her.

It was so strong I pulled out my camera but I knew I was too far away for her to show up in the picture. That was the last time we saw her but I have absolutely no doubt my French Tortoise made it to Santiago.

Day 6 Estella to Los Arcos

Today's haul was 13.4 miles (21.5km) from Estella to Los Arcos. All in all we've had it really good so far.

We seriously can't complain! I've seen a few people who look like they are in pain and have every right to complain and I've seen a few people who probably would have complained no matter what...Making me wonder what some people think they signed up for?..

"Really? You thought walking 15 miles a day, in the heat, for a month, staying in non-reservable rooms and eating foods you're completely unfamiliar with was going to be an easy thing?"

No of course not but some people look a little taken aback by the whole experience.

We, on the other hand, are living like kings. We have really splurged and gotten great rooms, great food and have absolutely no right to complain!

I feel extremely fortunate and grateful. I can't believe tomorrow will mean we have been walking for one week, CRAZY! I saw a group of people celebrating their last day today.

They were a group who had come to do just the first 6 days of the Camino and I thought "Wow I'm glad I'm not going home right now". Don't get me wrong I'm very homesick but the journey has just begun. Its several days before you even begin to start talking with the Camino (if that makes sense) in the beginning it's all just hard work and nervous energy, now you begin to settle in and the real journey begins.

This is the view from our room

...and of all our clothes hanging out to dry. The woman at the front desk assured me they had a clothes dryer but it turned out not to be working. So air dry we did (again)... Sigh.

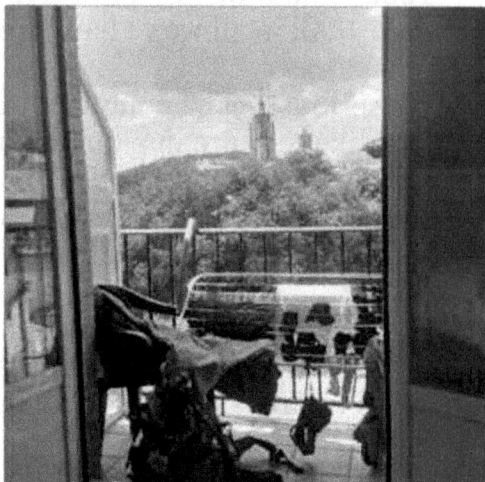

We left Estella just as the sun was coming up this morning.

Almost immediately we were greeted with the first of two surprises for the day.

The vino fountain! The famous wine fountain (Fuente del Vino) can be found at Bodegas Irache.

Here pilgrims are invited to drink until it's gone for the day. We were told it was only flowing from 8am-8pm but we were surprised to find it available at 6:30 this morning. A little too early for wine but we each had a sip (even Tony... whoa!)

The second surprise/treat for the day was a mobile food truck.

We pulled into one village this morning and the cafe wasn't open yet so we were very disappointed and continued on hoping the food truck, we had heard about, would be available... and it was! Very cool experience to be able to eat breakfast out in the middle of farm land in Spain

Then we entered Los Arcos and had a lovely lunch...

We're headed to Viana tomorrow marking 1 week and nearly 100 miles (161km)... woo hoo!

Day 7 Los Arcos to Viana

Today felt very easy (thank goodness) a little less than 12 miles (apx 19k) from Los Arcos to Viana...

I would like it to be noted in the annals of history that I, Molli, was the one who suggested "taking it easy" today and shortening the recommended route from a tough day of 17.3 miles (28km) down to 12... yes me... those of you who know me just fell over backwards, but it's true!

We took it easy today and got to Viana very early. This will give us a little more time to acclimate to 17, 18 and 20 mile days coming up soon.

Although the walk was shorter it was packed with beauty nonetheless. We left at 6am

The view as you approach Sansol The golden fields are spectacular!

Today was funny because as we left town we were walking through vineyards and being attacked by mosquitoes (the first we've encountered).

They were relentless! Generally with the mosquitoes, I'm familiar with, as long as you keep moving (walking fast or running) they won't bother you. These though... we were power walking and they could care less! They were biting us anyway. I felt like I was doing some kind of crazy new Jazzercise or Zumba because I was walking as fast as I could while flailing my hat, all about, trying to deter them. It was fairly successful but a little exhausting. The mosquito cloud lasted about an hour and we kept praying for the sun to come up hoping that would get rid of them. It seemed to work.

As we leave each small village there is usually a cemetery.

A little eerie but I had to grab a pic because they're at the edge of each village you pass through.

As we passed through one small village today a local woman was cracking

almonds. We stopped because she had a small table of things for sale and I wanted a hard boiled egg.

We paid and she gave Tony this handful of almonds, just because. How sweet is that?

The scenery was wonderful walking along today... (Please visit our blog for more pictures because I hate not being able to show them to you all here).

We came upon this little hut. You see these every now and then. Believe it or not these are shelters you can sleep in.

Alas we did not choose the rock hut.

We opted to "rough it" again today by staying in a palace that has been converted into a hotel "Palacio de Pujadas".

From our room we can see the city of Logrono, far out in the distance, (population 155,000) which we'll be passing through tomorrow.

Today we also opted to mail some things home. We packed really light but we still brought a couple items that have ended up being unnecessary. We sent home one sleeping bag and a rain jacket. I still have my rain poncho but the jacket seems redundant and it's been warm. If you find you really need something you can always re-buy it in one of the towns. Every pound you can get off your back is a good thing.

Coming into Viana today you could tell things were different. The people here are lively and beautiful. The town is not as sleepy as some of the villages we have walked through. With the exception of Pamplona we keep asking "where is everybody?"

Not here though. This place is vibrant and the Churches here are definitely some of the most beautiful I've been in.

I have noticed every church on the Camino (and there are a lot of them) has it's own "vibe". I really felt good in this one, Iglesia de Santa Maria. When I walked in I was literally brought to tears and was immediately drawn right up the center towards the altar and in front of a statue of Christ.

This is from the vantage point of kneeling below the figure looking up

Today my thoughts drifted to my sister Rose. I dedicated my walk, today, to her and I was hoping she could feel the love I was sending her and how grateful

I am she is taking care of our puppies at home... I know it's not easy and I hope she knows how much we appreciate it.

So I lit a candle for her and whenever I'm in a Catholic Church I can't help but think of my grandmother Rose Mary and so

I always light a candle for her.

This Church was interesting. They had an electronic candle so you put in coins to make them light up.

Ahhh technology has even made it here...

This is looking up inside the ancient ruins of the Church of St. Peter (San Pedro). The one right outside our hotel window.

Another short day tomorrow... Rain is in the forecast. Weather has been gorgeous so far but I wouldn't be opposed to some beautiful late afternoon thunderstorms!

Ultreia!

Day 8 Viana to Navarrete over the 100 mile mark

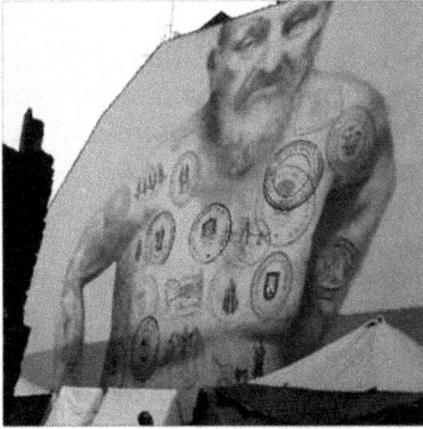

Isn't that a fantastic mural?

Those are the stamps you get along the way to complete your Pilgrims Passport.

You have to get a stamp, for every night you are on the Camino, to receive your Compostela in Santiago.

Today we walked a touch over 13 miles (apx 22k), from Viana to Navarrete, via the city of Logrono (pop. 155,000... Big City!)

We had some rain... which was a nice break from the heat. It allowed us to start a little later and we treated ourselves to the buffet at our Hotel.

The buffet was delicious at Palacio de Pujadas and only 3.5 Euro when added on to our hotel stay.

That's one of the strange things about the tourist end of the Camino, How much you pay for something is not a good indicator of what you're going to get. We have paid 5 Euro for a slice of toast and 3 Euro for a delicious buffet of meats, eggs, omelets, toast, cereal, juice, fruit, etc.

We are learning slowly but surely... the municipal albergue might be 10 Euro per person, where you're going to be crushed onto bunk beds and communal bathrooms. While a private room, in a hotel, might be 15 Euro per person.

We have also noticed a lot of the pilgrims seem to have come here with presupposed rules and conditions "I will only stay in the municipal albergues", "I will eat Pilgrim meals only". A pilgrims meal is 10 Euro per person and always includes your choice of chicken, fish, beef or pork and fries, with dessert and first course of several different options including ensalata mixta (salad). However just down the way you can get off the Pilgrim's menu for almost exactly the same price.

A good lesson in life "why are you making up rules for yourself?" Look around there are probably many other options but we build ourselves boxes, we feel safe within, and no matter how much you suffer (how bad that meal is) you stay there. There's a Camino lesson in there somewhere.

Last night I woke up in the middle of the night and decided I was going to show you the myriad of "signs" you follow along the way. As I'm sure you can tell, by now, the Camino de Santiago is a well marked path... Particularly the Camino Francés (the 500 mile route, from the South of France, we're on).

There is no getting lost on this trail... they are going to see to that! And so all along the way there are arrows, signs, etchings, paintings and statues pointing out "the way".

It's really cool... and we thought we would share some of those with you.

These were taken all along the path today and this is a tiny fraction of what was out there... In each of these pictures there is a sign or symbol pointing "the way"... can you find it in each picture? They show up really good on our blog www.PairOfGringos.com

When you get to big cities, it feels like you are in a very easy scavenger hunt... Sometimes ridiculously easy so you start to wonder what are they trying to do here... Out arrow each other or what?

This-a-way...

and That-a-way

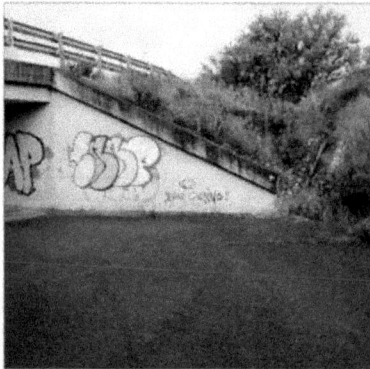

A little graffiti arrow for you...

Can you believe the pain staking measures taken to put up all these arrows across an entire Country?

Every tree along this path has an arrow painted on it.

The red and white painted lines symbolize the Camino Francés . Occasionally you'll see these in addition to the yellow arrows.

You get the idea... there are a lot of signs. They really take great care of the peregrinos (pilgrims) but that's understandable when you consider that many, in fact, most of the villages we pass through economy's are based on the Camino and it's Pilgrims.

"The truth hurts, yes...
but the lies are killing us."
Harrit

"the truth will set you free."
Jesus

Speaking of signs...

this is a sign we saw last night at a cool little tea shop in Viana called "Chill Cafe". The owners are from Walnut Creek, Ca. and we had a great visit with them... Super nice people Lauren and Terri, his wife, hooked us up with not only amazing "fennel" tea (something I've never had and really enjoyed) but also called and made arrangements for our accommodations the following night in Navarrete (without us even asking, they just offered... Super sweet!).

Meeting them was just one of those "Camino accidents". We were wandering around, with an hour to spare, before we were supposed to meet James for dinner, wondering what we should do and I was drawn into their store because I liked the message on this sign, and wanted a picture, and that's how we met and they hooked us up!

Because of Lauren and Terri making that call we got a great place in Navarrete, "El Cantaro", and that albergue owner was super nice and sent us off to a delicious lunch at "El Molino"... it's like a long link in a chain of following good signs!

This tripped me out, as we came into Logrono... Remember how we said "there's always a cemetery"? Well the big cities have big cemeteries and this one had a municipal crematorium attached, with the fire stack visible to the public, right out in the open.

They have a different relationship with death here. They're not trying to hide the fact that we die... as we so antiseptically do in the U.S.

It would serve us well to not attempt to hide from death. Get comfortable with it. It's inevitable and yet we do our best to ignore this huge portion of life.

I'm thinking of using this graffiti art as a muse for the tattoo I'll be getting in Santiago.

That's all for today.. Just keep walking and following the signs!

Day 9 Navarrete to Najera... short day

Today we had planned on doing a 20+ mile day to make up for shortening our route, the last couple days, but we woke up to pouring rain and decided to keep it short and not stress... What's the rush?... Santiago will be there. We walked in the most rain we've had so far...

We woke up at 5:30am to head out and after about 3 miles (5k) we took a very short side trek to end up in a little town called Ventosa for a breakfast break... There I had the best coffee, I've had so far, at this little cafe... (appropriately named) "Buen Camino".

While I was sitting in there I suddenly felt odd and I looked around and thought "I don't feel like I'm on the Camino right now" then I realized it was the first time, in over a week, I had been in a modern building. Funny how you can sense the difference.

Here are some random pictures we took along the way...

Rocks are a big thing here... Stacking them... Praying with them. I will never look at a rock the same way again.

Windy and Rainy...

Commercial Wineries...

Funny huts...

Rocks and arrows,
Arrows and Rocks...

The path today was
primarily through
vineyards... lots and lots
of grapes. I tried to take
a picture of the soil
because I wanted to
show how red and fertile
it is. The churned up
soil, is so thick, it sits a foot or more off the ground

And this was my Camino gift today... There was a heart in

the clouds. I was
walking alone,
deep in
meditation and I
looked up to see
this break in the
clouds... to me it
was unmistakably
a heart and I felt
so much love it
took my breath
away.

As we neared
Najera we all had
to use the
restroom. You feel guilty using a cafe's bathroom (or as
they call them water closets) without buying something so
we end up buying a lot of things we didn't really need.

Here we tried a couple little tapas in exchange for the use
of their potty.

The lady behind the counter laughed at me because I was trying, in my broken spanglish, to buy some biscuits that you get for free with your coffee. I didn't want coffee I just wanted the little cookies for Tony.

She finally acquiesced and made up a price for me... (We get laughed at a lot here :-)

We arrived in Najera (pop. 8500) a little before noon. This has been my favorite church and favorite hotel room so far.

The church is the Monastery of Santa Maria de La Real... unbelievable! We got into town so early we had to waste some time before we could check into our hotel and so we walked straight to the Monasterio. I have started to really look forward to peeking into the big churches in each town (every town has one). 4 Euro to enter (they haven't charged up until now) we paid our Euro and then we were blown away!

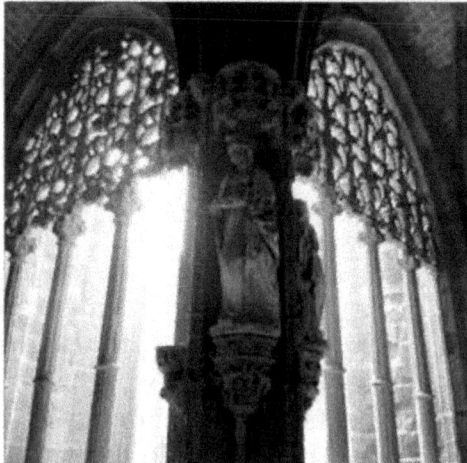

The pictures I took aren't going to do it justice...

Besides being beautiful there are tombs inside that date back to 1044 and older.

The two figures, on either side of this photo, are statues depicting Don Garcia and Dona Estefania, the founders of the monastery.

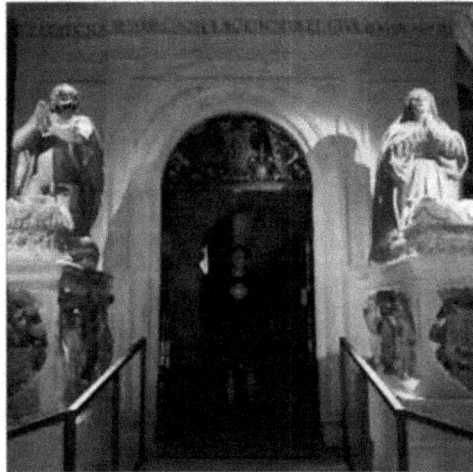

Legend has it that in 1044 Don Garcia went out hunting and followed a partridge into a cave. While inside the cave it is said Don Garcia had a vision...

The monastery is built on the very sight of that cave... Legend has it when Don Garcia got to the back of the cave he saw a vision of the Virgin Mary with a bell on one side, on the other a lamp, and in the middle a vase of white

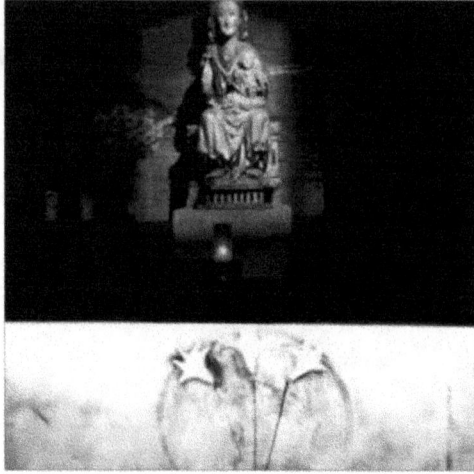

lilies. The picture on the left is what you see when you enter the cave now.

So you enter this really eerie space and inside they have the most beautiful altar and a huge bouquet of white lilies and it smells AMAZING... (the last thing you would expect to smell in that little room).

It's really beautiful I wish I could give you smell-a-vision so you could experience how wonderful the experience of stepping into this little cave is. 4 Euro yes totally worth it!

To make it all even more magical, while we were in the Church, it was thundering and pouring outside so it was very nice to be sheltered by the huge monastery. We heard some crazy thunder crashes and saw lightning so we were very glad we had opted for a short day and we weren't out in those elements!

Then we checked out a little place for lunch, bought some bags of ice for our feet, and checked into our hotel for the night, Hotel Ciudad de Najera, very nice!

The view from our room overlooks the same rock the monastery is built into... too cool!

Tomorrow is Santo Domingo de la Calzada another somewhat large town (pop. 6600)

Wish us no rain... I mean sun :-) for the 13 miles ahead.

Ultreia!

Day 10 Oops! Najera to Santo Domingo

Today's walk from Najera to Santo Domingo felt like walking through a bouquet of flowers.

The fields were so beautiful and I ADORE THE POPPIES... at least I think that's what these red flowers are that have covered our entire journey so far. We had 13.2 miles (21.3 k) through rolling farm land and vineyards...

One of James's friends sent him this text "Cada momento es unico, y nunca vuelva." and I believe that translates to "every moment is unique and never again" that is the Camino to a tee. The same day James received that text Tony was saying "this is a unique experience" and I couldn't agree

more. I just don't know anywhere else in the world where you could experience anything like this; To be taken care of on a path of 500 miles (over 800 k) by entire cities and villages.

An entire nation facilitating your safe and comfortable journey while walking through their home... It brings tears to my eyes... Priceless!

Of course it's not all perfect... Tony keeps getting yelled at for touching the fruit. You see in the U.S. we touch all the fruit to decide which pieces we want. Here you're supposed to let the store owners hand you what they want to sell you (that's a hard habit to break... but we're working on it).

We sometimes get separated from the locals, to eat. I don't think that's anything to take offense to. I think it's just a timing thing. They're in the bar and we're eating at odd times. and today to top it off the waitress actually sprayed us with room fragrance. UM... I really don't think we smell yet but apparently I'm wrong... ha ha ha!

Speaking of stinking... We had to fix this problem (which we did before the restaurant occurrence)... Tony's Vibrams stink!... He doesn't generally have foot odor but when he wears his Five Finger Vibrams and they get wet... they wreak! So we bought bleach and we're trying to fix it, otherwise they're getting tossed (because it really isn't him... it's the shoes). We love Five Fingers but the smell is an issue.

Then I pulled a REALLY bonehead move! I left half of my clothes in our last hotel in Najera. I'm not usually a scatterbrain and we've been so careful, so I keep trying to figure out how I managed to leave a skirt, pair of underwear and two tank tops in the room? Considering all I have left, now, is my hiking clothes and 1 pair of sweat shorts. Geesh... how did I manage that? I don't believe in accidents but I'm trying to get the meaning behind that one... I guess it will come later.

Considering how long the journey is I think you'd have to say it's as close to perfect as you can get.

The food has been fine (getting a little redundant)... Lots of Atun (tuna for Tony) and today a goat cheese salad with balsamic for me.

We are in another great casa rural, El Molino de Floren, I LOVE IT HERE!!! the rooms are adorable... We have been so fortunate with beautiful accommodations.

We haven't been into the Cathedral yet, it's open till 8 to visitors so we're going over, in a bit. You'll have to wait for those pics later but I'm excited to see this one... (Although there is a charge to go in. If they keep charging we will be forced to pick and choose because 34 days of anything adds up).

I'm looking forward to seeing this one because it has great lore behind it. This is the cathedral with the chickens inside it. The story is a fantastical one. The story has it that a pilgrim family stopped here on their way to Santiago. and the inn keepers daughter took a liking to the son of the family but he did not reciprocate so in retaliation she put a silver goblet in his backpack and reported it missing. The next day the boy was arrested.

The parents left town and came back to find their son had been hung but he was not dead. They ran to the sheriff and told him their son was still alive. The sheriff was in the middle of eating dinner when the parents found him. He didn't believe them and said "your son is no more alive than the cock I'm about to eat" at that moment the fowl leapt off his plate and began crowing. Whereupon the sheriff ran to the gallows and released him.

Isn't that a great story?

To commemorate the story they have a rooster and hen in the back of the cathedral, which I am very much looking forward to seeing.

How the Camino works its magic...
Stripped Away

As we have had a little time now to come back and process what happened to us on the Camino we can see some of what happens to you (or at least happened to us) out there.

It strips you down to your bare essentials. You are reminded over and over again, in the guide books and blogs, to take as little as possible. "To keep your pack light". Logically this makes sense because you have to carry your belongings on your back for 30+ days and if you don't want to end up without a broken back, knees, feet, etc. You should heed this advice. But the Camino is also going to do it for you... Strip you away that is.

It removes what is unnecessary from your life. Possessions make you think and worry about keeping those things safe. The more you have, the more energy you spend thinking about what you have. The more of your attention is taken away from source.

I thought I had packed as little as possible and yet on Day 10 I "left behind" an entire outfit. I had brought 3 outfits; #1 My hiking outfit, #2 a pair of sweatshorts and sweatshirt, to change into once we finished hiking each day, and a third outfit. The one I considered my "cute" outfit... A skirt and two layered tank tops. On day 10 this outfit... let's just say... "disappeared". I use that word because of the mystery behind it's disappearance. It is almost impossible to have left behind an entire outfit, in the room, when we packed so diligently, each morning, and Tony was extremely thorough in checking that we didn't leave things behind. Leaving it there is pretty much impossible.

I believe now the Camino stripped me of this outfit because it was an "excess" I did not require.

PairOfGringos.com

You are there to be simple... to be stripped down to the essentials. Little entertainment (besides the landscape you are hiking by), no flashy food, no deciding what to wear... Just get up each morning, put on your hiking clothes, pack your back pack and leave.

There are no bills to pay...

No job to go to...

No children to get your attention...

You have one job and that is to get up and walk. There isn't even much thinking to be done because the arrows are so painstakingly laid out for you, there is almost no need for a map.

Just the basics; fill up your water bottle, walk to the next village, eat something, go to the bathroom and fill up your water bottle again.

After that it's just you and your thoughts.

What other time in your life do you get the opportunity to be that quiet and without distraction?

This is what we believe makes the Camino so special. It is an opportunity for God to get your, nearly undivided, attention.

The gift of the Camino is in the monotony...

God is always there... but we are too distracted with our everyday lives, our "to do lists", and our keeping up with Jones' to see.

We become distracted and we turn away from the voice that is speaking to our soul. We have to stop and listen and the easiest way to do that is to strip away what you don't need...To stop and say "enough!"

The business of my everyday life was keeping me from hearing God. I kept saying "I'm too busy" the Camino gave me the gift of being able to shut up and listen.... really for the first time in my life.

Day 11 Santo Domingo to Belorado

Today the flowers were so beautiful I was afraid I would never make it to the destination because I couldn't stop taking photos...

I would imagine a photographer would go absolutely mad on the Camino.

There is so much to take pictures of and they would want to wait to get the perfect photo and I can't imagine how frustrating that would be...

luckily for me I have no artistic talent and therefore I just snap away and what you get is what you get :-)

Almost immediately, this morning, there was a field of these white flowers. Then lots more of my reddish, orange poppies... *Ok so this is a funny sidenote* (I just asked our hospitaleros what the name of the white flower is and it turns out it's also in the poppy family and they're all opiates produced for the pharmacies. How hysterical is that?! Boy did my bubble just burst. Oh well they're still beautiful)

The side of the road was paved with a myriad of wildflowers. As we neared Granon I was watching Tony and James walk ahead of me and I was picturing them as little boys walking along, playing.

They were so cute and I started a meditation where you just hug the person in your mind. First people you love and are close to, that's easy.

Then even people you have issues with until you can hug everyone in your heart with no hesitation.

It's a delightful meditation and leaves you feeling very much at peace.

Then things got funny as we were heading into the village I looked down and saw a crawdad... It seemed so out of place here in farmlands. I cracked up and called the boys back to look at it because they had missed it. I asked "ok who was picturing lobster?" We seem to be manifesting things so fast out here I figured somebody must have been craving lobster or thinking about Louisiana or something...

Do you remember the scene in the movie Ghostbusters, at the end of the movie, where they say you have to be careful what you think of because that's what's going to come back and annihilate the city? That's kind of like what's happening out here, everything you picture, you manifest, very quickly. It's really bizarre.

This is the crawdad after James pissed it off. He tossed a rock to make sure it was alive and it reared up and said "Are you threatening me?... sorry little buddy... Go back to your Camino. We'll leave you alone now.

Today was definitely creepy, crawly day...

We've had giant slugs and lots and lots of snails, the whole way.

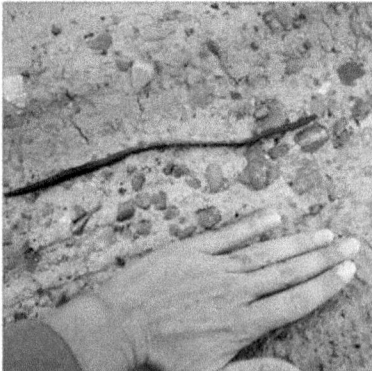

Add to that giant worms (I guess with fields this big you need worms to match), Giant bumble bees and now a crawdad. I hope that's it for creepy crawly's "

Lots more signs counting down the miles (kilometers) to go...

About 5k (3miles) outside of Belorado we came upon this restaurant, Casa Leon.

We had a delicious little snack and if I had an unlimited bank account I would have sent a gift of the artisan foods home to all of you.

The food was pure art!

Funny story about this restaurant... I ordered toast with tomato and olives on top and the gentlemen argued with my order (very politely) insisting that I have Jamon (which of course is a delicacy here they are very proud of).

This has happened a couple times where I order, one thing, and they basically say "oh no you need to try this instead". I love it... it shows such pride and I just eat whatever they bring... It's (usually) delicious.

We made our way into Belorado just as it began to rain (perfect timing) and found an adorable hotel rural, Casa Verde Ancho.

Then we had lunch and made our way up to the caves... Oh yes I did make Tony hike up there after a five hour hiking day... Heck yeah!

Check out the view of the nests on the Church from this high up... pretty spectacular to be eye level with them.

This is our office, for the day, where Tony is posting and texting with his sister Jan, right this moment, and where I'm writing this...

And this is the ridiculousness the sweet hotel owners have to deal with... on top of us smelly pilgrims, now these guys just rode up.

There was an off road bike race today and these guys are, filthy, covered in mud! Staying here they asked if they could get hosed off before coming in... I asked if they minded if I took their photo and they were happy to pose.

It's one surprise after another, and around every corner, on the Camino...

Ultreia until tomorrow...

Day 12 Belorado to Ages... A little hilly and a little chilly

The sunrise as we left Belorado this morning... it's so weird to leave a new town every day.

Today was the coldest day we've had so far. If I had to guess I would say 55 degrees Fahrenheit. The rainy days have been rather humid so not as chilly as this one.

Our landscape changed a lot. Today we climbed into a forest and went through several tiny villages, most of which were closed because we came through so early.

The first town we entered was Tosantos. The really cool thing about this town is the Church built into the side of the cliffs

The Ermita Virgen de la Pena (Our Lady of the Cliff).

The next village was Villambistia and although everything was still closed as we walked through. We read, legend has it, if we dunked our heads in the town's fountain we would not be weary all day...

Well it woke us up that's for sure! We stopped several times today in cafes to warm up and have a cup of coffee.

While we were at the cafe I was telling James, my sister Laura's, "buy a donkey story" So I'll tell you the story now... Laura and I were training for a marathon and as you do at mile 15, or so, we were getting a little delirious and she said "do you want to just add another 2 miles on this week". I said "let's wait another mile and decide" and she responds back with... "yeah I guess if you buy that donkey you gotta ride it home" and so now that's our phrase whenever you've got a big decision.

"If you buy that donkey you gotta ride it home".

Well I told that story and not ten minutes further up the path guess what we crossed...

A donkey literally blocking the road!!!

We told you the Camino is a manifesting machine... So sista this picture is for you... Love you!

The climb today was through a forest with a summit of 3773 feet (1150 m)

At the summit there is a monument dedicated to the tragedy of the Spanish Civil War. A very somber spot.

San Juan de Ortega had a nice church.

I keep promising myself I will take a picture of everything we eat no matter how bad it is and

I'm always so starving when we sit down I have it half eaten before I remember...

Here's half of my lunch. Salami and bread...(literally that's it. It's not all roses out here :-) I had to track down some mustard just so it wouldn't be so dry and I could swallow it. and Tony's 8 banana peels. (Did I mention he's being a lot healthier than me out here?)

This is also the first time I had a beer with lunch and still had a few more miles to walk before our destination for the night. BIG mistake... between the heavy sandwich and beer my stomach was churning the rest of the walk into Ages... Yuck! Won't make that mistake again. No beer until we're in for the night.

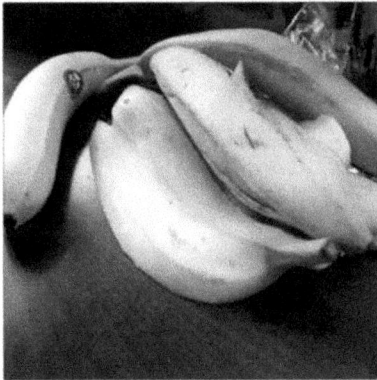

The great thing about this stop, Tony was able to help a guy from Colorado with some "Fab 5". It's really rewarding to be able to see people get back up on their feet out here.

It's so sad when an injury takes you out of the game especially here when it's a life long dream to be able to walk the Camino. 15 minutes and he was good to go... Gotta love the Fab 5! See (BeInstantlyBetter.com)

You're probably thinking "Oh let's see how cute their room is tonight." Oh no!

This one is a roughing it night... no privacy today.. our 4th room mate, is from Italy, ...

That's it for now... Ciao!

Day 13 Ages to Burgos

So tired... Can barely type... The exhaustion of 161 miles (261km) in 13 days is catching up to us. Toss in a horrible night's sleep and too many days of salami, in a row, and you've got a recipe for a crappy day! Sorry I'm going to whine for a second (I know, I know I have absolutely no right in the world to whine so I'll be brief).

My tummy doesn't feel good from such an unfamiliar diet... blah, blah, blah, whine, whine, whine...

Last night I ran out of contact lens solution and where we had stopped in Ages literally had nothing. But I brought extra contacts so I was able to switch them out. Most of the villages have had lots of farmacias so I thought Ages would too but alas no. Little did we know about 1 mile (2k) away was a cute town Atapuerca that would have had better lodging, better food, and my contact lens solution but you can't tell everything by trying to decipher a guidebook.

Luckily for us though we did not know that Atapuerca was bigger because we definitely would have gone there and that would have meant missing out on two good things about Ages... One we had a great conversation with a gentlemen who lives in the Ukraine and two we had quite the dinner theater going on at our Albergue, San Rafael.

The waiter was an absolute riot and kept us laughing out loud the whole meal. Worth giving up creature comforts for... I think.

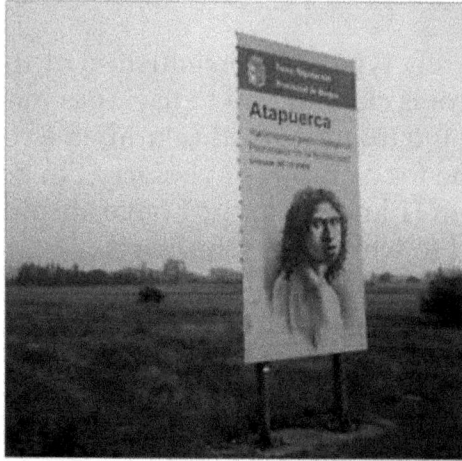

On the way out of Ages we passed through Atapuerca which is known as the site of our earliest ancestors.

The prehistoric caves of Atapuerca were deemed a World Heritage Site by UNESCO because the earliest human remains ever discovered in Europe were found here. WE did not get to see the caves however because it was 3k off the road... bummer!

As we climbed out of Atapuerca we summited Cruz de Matagrande 3543 ft. (1080m) with a cross indicating the top.

Our journey today was taking us to Burgos which is a large city and one thing I was pleased with is I caught myself before I fell into the "to do list" trap.

I could have easily fallen into letting my thoughts run wild with things to do once we got to Burgos; laundry, contact lens solution, stocking up on things we'll need for the upcoming crossing of the Meseta, instead of staying in the NOW and enjoying every step of this journey. I forced myself to quiet my mind, relax and stay in the Camino not in the future. It was lovely and because of it I deeply enjoyed the first several miles of the day.

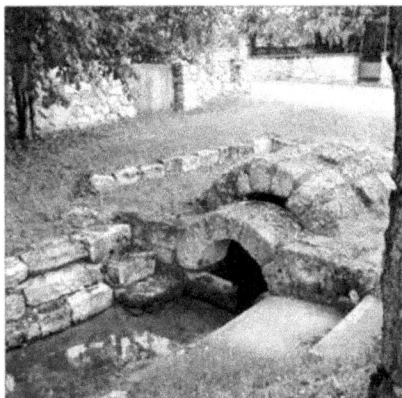

This is an ancient Roman fountain that still functions... how cool is that?

Look I realized we're the people running on the signs here... Watch out for peregrinos! I swear every time I see one of these signs someone almost gets hit. I guess we're not getting it.

I had taken a lot of time to study the route going into Burgos today.

Guidebooks clearly tell you to avoid the main route and use an unmarked scenic byway through a park instead. So I probably spent at least an hour making sure I knew how to get us there..

Weellllll... We started down the correct path to avoid the city streets and not a quarter mile in Tony and James yell to me that "it's too muddy" and they want to turn around and go the other way. I WAS FURIOUS...(oh well there went all that morning peace). All that work and these two wouldn't walk through some mud to avoid 6 miles of hard pavement.

Look, it may not sound like that big of a deal but pavement hurts when you're feet are tired and when someone has, painstakingly, laid out a plan because you told them you would do whatever they suggested.... then expect to get some attitude when you change the plans on a dime.

Ok then I let it go and we walked 6 miles on this...

In order to avoid this:

Does anybody remember the 70's sitcom *Alice* about the diner?... "Well kiss my grits!"

I will give them this... It was very muddy and slippery but the terrain out here changes on a dime. Enough said. Some of the signs along the way, into Burgos, were pretty entertaining though!

We got to our hotel without much further ado and then I promptly started the things on my now complete "to do list".

Lunch was delicious James had chicken and fries, Tony another Ensalata mixta... and me another Goat cheese salad... and agua in a very pretty bottle.

Great news the room has a bath tub... woo hoo! Time to soak my, only slightly aching feet. They really are holding up well.

Tomorrow we enter the Meseta, a stretch of land dreaded by some because of it's lack of trees and sparse accommodations. I'm actually looking forward to it because they say it feels like you're walking through the sky. LOVE IT!

If you don't hear from us don't worry it just means no wifi but we'll see, fingers crossed.

(P.s. to our Boot Campers back home... We hope you had an awesome workout! I sure do miss doing exercises other than walking!!!! I tried to knock out a couple pushups for you all but alas this unhealthy diet is starting to catch up with me!)

Ultreia!

Day 14 Let the Death begin... Burgos to Hontanas

Woo hoo!!! We made it to the 2 week point.. very cool! Today was 20 miles (31.4k) and it felt great! Most likely because, today, we died. As I mentioned earlier, the Camino breaks into three quadrants; Life, Death and Re-birth. Today we left Life and walked onto the Meseta which begins the Death portion of the Camino and it feels wonderful! We left behind the hustle and bustle of Burgos this morning at 6am.

As the sun rose we passed the Catedral de Santa Maria XIII. I'm really sorry I missed getting a chance to walk through this magnificent place... at least we got the opportunity to walk past the outside of it this morning. WOW!

Burgos ended up being a fun town. We were able to sight see a bit as we walked around getting errands done. We had our clothes washed at a dry cleaners, Alba Tintorerias. The woman who owned the place was a real "camino angel". I wasn't sure she would be able to get them done in time for us to pick them up that evening, because it was already late, and there was no way we could wait to get them in the morning but she was very accommodating and rushed them through for us. So sweet. It's these little gestures that end up making such a difference.

That evening we had a delicious Italian meal at La Mafia...

Here are the appetizers... I forgot to take a picture of the rest (I'm always too hungry to remember). I had the best glass of red wine (but I forgot to take a picture of the bottle to remember the name) later when we got the check Tony's water was more expensive than my wine... (He he he that's a first!)

The hotel we stayed in, Norte Y Londres, was centrally located, right in the heart of it all, and very nice but as we were leaving town we passed Hotel abba Burgos and if I came here again I would want to give it a try. It's very close to the Cathedral and looked quite appealing. It is at the far end of town though so that would mean a longer walk into Burgos the previous day...

It's always hard to come in and out of the big cities and leaving Burgos was no exception. There was a bit of construction, re-routing us momentarily, but no big deal.

We did have to navigate a bit of freeway though... VROOM!

Two way rush hour traffic and peregrinos...that'll wake you up in the morning!

So does walking 6 miles before your first coffee and breakfast in Tardajos...

Breakfast tasted exactly like a Jack-n-the-box sourdough breakfast sandwich and that egg thing at the top of the picture is called a "tortilla patata".

It's basically a baked egg and potato omelet and we eat them almost every day here. (Did I mention there's not a lot of variety... 2 weeks in and the novelty begins to wane)

And here's Tony with his bag o' bananas... He's such a healthy boy!

I haven't talked about the water here but it's amazing. I can't remember the last time I drank tap water. It's so weird to be able to turn on a faucet and drink the water and have it not taste like a hose or chlorine. And the water pressure here is absolutely amazing... it'll knock you clear out of the shower... No droughts here!

Then we were off to our last little village Rabe de las Calzadas before we hit the Meseta..

And there it is, at last, the infamous Meseta!

Just before we made the climb I saw a huge field of my red poppies and I thought... "that's them saying good bye to me". They knew how much I loved them and they may not be up there. I thought that's death right? Giving up all the things in this world, for the beauty in the next and the tears began.

A little rise up onto a mesa and then you're at the top... known as "Cuesta matamulas" (Mule killing incline) because of how steep the decline is on the other side.

Tony and I were holding hands and I realized we were going to see "death" together and I was not afraid. It was beautiful... This was a very powerful moment for me. I don't know whether it was conjured up in my head, due to my anticipation of seeing the meseta or not, but it was powerful nonetheless and I could sense there was a lot more going on during this trip than you could see on the surface.

The moment was fleeting however because very quickly we came into another town and it was back to reality.

We came into Hornillos del Camino and used the facilities, at a very nice man's store, had our Pilgrim's passports stamped and we were off... back into nature.

After walking a long while we detoured a tiny bit off the path to San Bol. Which boasts one tiny albergue and a very cold pool to stick your feet into.

Rumor has it if you soak you're feet here you won't have feet issues the rest of the way. I will add this caveat to that... Putting your feet in ice cold water is one of the best things you can do for aching feet... IF (and I do mean IF!) you are done for the day and can let them rest. Cramming your feet back into

shoes and walking, two more miles, is absolutely not going to take the pain away... In fact it's much worse for awhile :-)
The San Bol albergue is absolutely adorable and if we come back we will stay here for a night for sure!

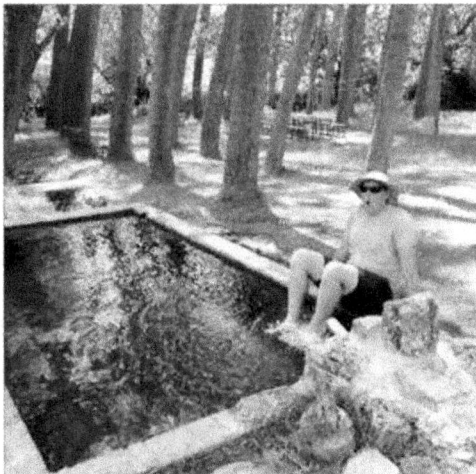

How these peregrinos look is how we felt yesterday. Actually the guy in white was our Italian bunk mate in Ages. He's fine, he's just on the phone. I don't know what's up with the other two...

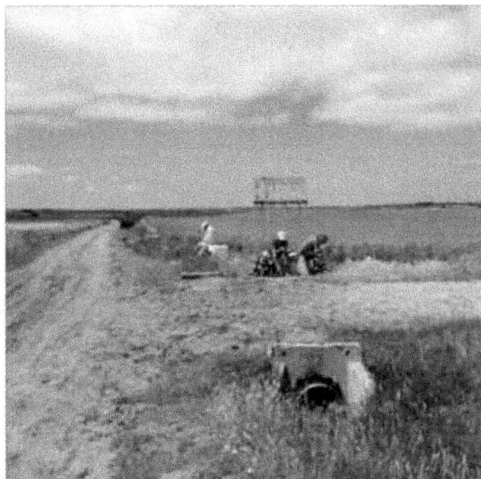

I saw blue butterflies today (or moths whatever they were, they were pretty)..

Hontanas is our stopping point for today. It may look weird, in the picture, but it's really cool. Lots of character in this ramshackle village and we have a sun roof in our room so we'll finally be able to see the stars.

We can never stay up late enough to see the stars... It doesn't get dark till after 10!

More death tomorrow...

Bring it on Ultreia!

P.s. the water just shut off in our building so no shower right now, YIKES! But we have WiFi (weee feee Yaaaayyyyy)

Day 15 Hontanas to Boadilla del Camino

Can you decipher this code; OW....O...w....ow.... ow.... ow.... ow... (insert explicative here).... Ow?

Ummm in case you didn't get that I hurt a little today.

My right shin (aka anterior tibialis) hurts like a son of a gun!!!! As soon as I woke up this morning and took my first step, stabbing shooting pain, all the way through the 17.7 miles to Boadilla del Camino... but who gives a Sh--!!! We're 214.7 miles (345km) into this baby... woo hoo!!!

No seriously here's my problem; My athletic background is so engrained, I have learned to pretty much continue through anything. The last 5 miles of today I had to have a serious discussion with myself "Self this is not a race. There is no wrong *way* to do this! Take a cab if you need to".

And if there had been a taxi I would have gotten in but we were in the middle of nowhere.

I did however allow Tony to take my pack (a huge step for me because I did not want him to suffer and get sore because of me) and I ran. Yes it may sound absolutely ridiculous but the gait of running is entirely different than the heel strike of walking, and running did not hurt, in fact it felt really good! And so I, went ahead and looked like an idiot, and ran the last 5 miles. With everyone pointing to my back and asking "Where's your pack?" and me replying "My husband is carrying it for me" and them gasping at me...

Yes I ignored it and ran anyway. Had a great time, reserved a room for Tony and I, made sure James had a room for the night, and went back to the end of the trail to lead them to our albergue.

Now ice, rest, elevation, and as soon as I finish this some serious Fab 5 and I'll be good to go tomorrow, unless the Camino has more of a humbling lesson in store for me :-) In spite of the pain; which I dealt with by "tapping", being extremely aware of my posture (which has been horribly crunched forward due to the pack), Saying "yes" to it, and finally running, today was a great day.

Last night without realizing it we ate dinner at a place I had read about and wanted to stop, Santa Brigida Albergue, in Hontanas, it was a delicious treat and so fun to eat somewhere we had read about in our research. We did not stay there but we did eat, along with a nest of 5 baby birds. Right above our head's, whose mom was feeding them as we ate our dinner. Too Cute!

Sunrise this morning over the Convento de San Anton
I felt so fortunate to be here at the moment the sun was peeking through that arch...
breathtaking! This moment was my Camino gift for the day...

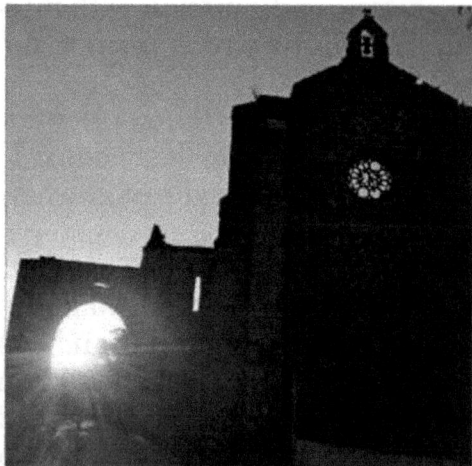

Then about 6 miles (9.4k) after we started, out for the day, we had breakfast in Castrojeriz next to Iglesia de Santa Maria del Manzano

The castle on the hill is said to be Roman, founded by none other than Julius Caesar, to protect the roads to Galicia's lucrative gold mines and Roman roads still exist leaving Castrojeriz.

This land used to be swamp and the Romans created this bridge and roadway to get through the marshy area...

Then we began our ascent...
To the top Alto de Mostelares..

and down the other side...

PairOfGringos.com

Just before entering the village of Itero de Vega we came across the unassuming and lovely San Nicolas Chapel.

This is a quiet Albergue known for the ritual of washing Pilgrim's feet every evening. This is another sweet spot like San Bol, yesterday, where if you wanted a quiet, more peaceful, journey you would definitely want to make this one of your stays... The hosts were lovely people offering free coffee this morning.

Then it was lunch in Itero de Vega. Where we were "pitched" by a couple, competing restaurants, to eat at their establishment. Entrepreneur-ism is alive and well on the Camino...
love it!

After lunch I got to see a herd of sheep, with two working dogs, a shepherd, and a mule... How freakin' cool is that? Keep in mind I'm a girl from busy Southern California. The only herds we see are herds and herds of cars on the freeways! The sheep took up the entire road and I stepped off into the farm fields to get out of the way but one peregrino stood right in the middle, of the road, and the sheep went all around her like a rock in the middle of a river. I was so bummed I wanted a do over... "hey I want to do that come back so I can try again :-)"

Then on to our stop for today Boadilla del Camino and the fantastic, albergue En El Camino. We were referred to this stop by our friends at Chill Cafe in Puente La Reina and boy is it cute! They have a typical shared bunk bed situation, in the albergue, as well as private rooms... woo hoo for private beds and showers... Yay!

When we arrived today we had snacks with a woman from Holland. Who has, over the past 4 years (on and off), hiked all the way here, from Holland, with her husband (and her Border Collie through most of it, although the doggy isn't with them now). So July 7th they will have completed their 4 year journey from Holland... WoW!

Okay I'm about to eat my necklace, I'm so hungry, so I'm going to go find some food... Good luck to me... dinner isn't for two more hours.

Ultreia! until tomorrow...

Day 16 Boadilla del Camino to Carrion de Los Condes

As promised the Meseta has been a little more desolate and boring than the previous days but today, three really cools things have happened (Four if you include my leg allowing me to walk... woo hoo!)

#1 Last night my sister Rose sent me a text message and mentioned wanting me to do a little "Camino manifesting" for her "perfect mate" so I was looking forward to setting that intention for the day...

First thing in the morning, I grabbed a rock off the ground, (People place rocks everywhere around here with an intention and prayer behind it) and I prayed she would "find her true heart's desire". I carried it with me for a couple hours and kept touching it in my pocket and refocusing on the intention "for her highest and best good". Then I started looking for a pretty place to set the rock.

This morning's walk started out following a really cool canal, the Canal de Castilla, which runs 1.8k all the way to Fromista

All morning, I looked and looked for a place to lay "Rose's rock" and kept thinking "No that's not pretty enough" or "That spot is too lonely" and then I saw a pretty stone cross sitting out in a golden wheat field and I thought it was nice but as I was debating

Tony yelled out "how about that spot for Rose's rock?" and pointed to the cross. I said I'd walk out there and check it out to see if it was the perfect spot or not. I got out there and burst into tears...

Not only had other people walked out into this field, to leave a stone, but right there was a paper rose...

Unbelievable. God is not impossible. You can't make this SHIT up! The Camino is a very interesting place... and "Rose you better watch out because someone or something is on it's way" :-)

Today felt a little bit more like a peregrino freeway... Now that we are getting a little closer to Santiago you start seeing more tour buses of people hopping on and off the Camino. It gets a little annoying because you feel like you've been working so hard and these people jump in and out of their bus, walk 3 miles and then stay in "your" hotels and albergues but that is not a fair way to look at it.

There is no wrong way to do the Camino. If you go down that route then it's a never ending loop. You could say we aren't depriving ourselves enough because we're not staying in only religious albergues, or not going to enough masses, or not flogging ourselves as we walk, etc, etc.

No matter how self righteous some people, like me, feel like being there are no rules (well technically there are see "The Rules" section of this book under Logistics)...

Granted they may not get much out of it but that's their Camino... It turns into just the "next" thing they get to chalk off their bucket list. The truth is you can do "the Camino" anywhere, yes the road is marked, and the towns hospitable, but the real journey is inside.

I see many people walking this path and getting nowhere but a few more miles down the road. The journey is in the monotony. In quieting your ego enough to hear what the Universe, God, (whatever you believe speaks to you) has been trying to tell you all along. You have to be quiet enough to hear that. You have to learn how to shut your self dialogue up and let the monotony of the walking, having nothing to do, nowhere to go, but forward, step after step, help you get to that quiet place. It can happen, for anyone, if you allow it. I suppose it could even happen on a bus.

Amongst the sparse fields today up popped the 2nd really cool surprise The Henderson's Oasis (just kidding it wasn't called that but our family will understand). This absolutely adorable albergue, *Amanecer albergue...* is like heaven on earth.

I mean literally there were dogs and geese and chickens, with baby chicks, and mules and ducks and everyone was just chilling out in the gardens. Cohabiting as if this was all completely normal. I have never seen so many animals so kosher with each other.

(okay there was one doggy who wanted to play with the geese and they weren't having it but everyone else was happy)

There's Tony happy as a clam in his hammock. It was a total hippie vibe at this albergue.

Around the back we saw a few of the sleeping quarters.... what a trip!

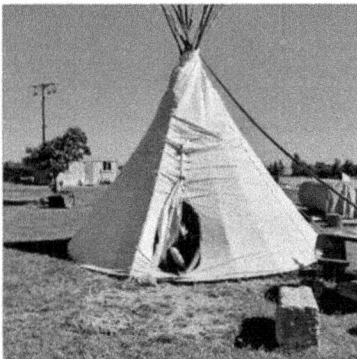

Of course Tony wanted to stay here but it was too early and I didn't want to sleep in that thing.. cute as it may be... (a note to my mom "Jmom I don't think we would have ever gotten you to leave this place... even the owner was a cool drink of tall hippie water... You would have loved it!")

After leaving here things out on "the way" had quieted down a little and it was a more peaceful walk into Carrion de los Condes .

I had walked with a much slower pace today, than I had on previous days, and that slower pace was much gentler on my leg (I know, I know I didn't listen to the dream... I was supposed to be walking slowly anyway) but today I did slow my pace so that worked well. The pain welled up a bit in the last 3 miles and I looked at the sign for the taxi service but something inside of me wouldn't let me do it. So I just put the whole concept, of riding in a car, out of my mind so it would no longer be an option and I accepted the pain. It almost turned into a meditation with the pain helping me to "tune in" deeper in some ways.

And of course the moment I became one with the pain and let go of trying to avoid it, it almost entirely disappeared. Isn't the mind a crazy, wonderful, thing!

The third awesome thing of the day was lunch... Yum! We have been so deprived of vegetables, but today we got a nice assortment. Mine was called the Queen's salad how cool is that name? and Tony had grilled vegetables. There was so much variety on each of our plates we were jumping for joy. I didn't know capers could be that big... at least I think that was a caper in the picture (12 o'clock on the plate). They were delicious!!!

Tonight we hope to see the "singing nuns" of Santa Maria.

Ultreia! until tomorrow...

Update on Rose... I'm not making this up...

I have done my best to be as real and forthright with, you, our readers, in the writing and documenting of our journey as possible. I would never make something up for the sake of sensationalism. This is a true account of our trip, not fiction... I'm not a talented enough writer to do a fictional account :-). So here is the outcome of the prayer for Rose.

3 days after I said that prayer and left that rock. The man who had broken up with my sister, just before we left. The man she had loved and wanted to marry, called her and said he had made a huge mistake. Told her "He loved her and wanted her back in his life".

You can't make this stuff up!

I could not believe what she was telling me on the phone. We didn't find out until O'Cebreiro many days later but when she told me I was floored!

Tony couldn't believe it either we both thought that relationship was long gone. Neither of us saw that coming.

Normally I would not pray for someone else because that's meddling. Life is each of our journey's. It's not my job to meddle in someone's life. The only reason I set the stone and the intention is because she commissioned me to do it. It was her action not mine.

I prayed with clear intention for her "highest and best good and the highest and best good of all involved". and I carefully set my intention with a clear mind... "For her true heart's desire".

Meaning I did not picture, a particular man, or scenario. I did not try to figure anything out. That is not our job.

Our job is to be clear about the outcome. Rose happy and fulfilled having the opportunity to truly love and be loved in her life was my prayer.

The How is not our job... the How is God's job. Just be clear and get out of the way. God is always answering... "Yes"... it's our Egos which block the way by thinking we have it figured out HOW it will come to us.

Lesson from the Camino... God does not work in Mysterious Ways

We've all heard the saying "God works in mysterious ways" but we completely disagree... God <u>does not</u> work in mysterious ways...

It's just not what our ego's would have come up with because we can never see the whole picture.

This is the problem with our minds... they are regularly wrong.

And yet because being wrong, in of and itself, is a threat not only are we wrong, we convince ourselves we're right. It's kind of funny when you really think about it. It's like a big vicious cycle. Some kind of huge cosmic joke...
But it's not a joke. It's how we are hard wired. We know we only use a small percentage of our brains capacity.

Here's what I believe the first portion of our mind is like an animal's. We react; Flight, fight and freeze. This is our first response to insure survival.

This is why we generally see what is wrong or negative about a situation first. If there is a potential threat our brain's will pick it out.

That's survival

Then we are computers... making calculations and decisions. We do this primarily based on our history. X happened before when I hit this switch so I can only assume X will happen again if I hit it now.

Or I saw Y happen when Sam hit that switch so I can only assume if I hit it Y will happen to me as well.

The brain's job is to calculate and attempt to figure things out and it uses past memory to do this.

This often results in being dead wrong. This cycle is what our minds go through day in and day out. Our minds are simply a calculator, a very advanced magnificent computer but a computer none the less. We are not our minds. In fact our minds get in the way with our connection to our true source, God.

I believe once you get past the animal in all of us, then get past the computer, you begin to uncover who we are at our source.

That urge to try and figure things out... to stress out endlessly and plan, plan, plan is all fodder for not trusting that God has the way covered.

When you are constantly stuck in listening, to those portions of the mind, you stop listening to your true source.

Anita Moorjani in her book, Dying to be Me, makes an analogy, I love. She compares life to being in a pitch dark room with only a flashlight for light. Because we can only see where we direct the light we can never make out the whole picture.

We are in the dark and we have to use other senses to see the entire picture. It's not going to come down to only what you can see.

Tony and I have a process we teach clients called "See it as Perfect". It's essentially a "feel-ization" exercise (meaning you have to incorporate your emotions). It works very well and one of the key steps in the process is; once you have taken a moment to experience the emotion of having already achieved your goal... What that "feels" like to already be there... then you let the whole thing go.

You let go of "how" your goal manifestation is going to come about. We call it "letting go of the how". This is an essential step because quite frankly your mind has no freaking idea "how" otherwise you would have already done it!!!

By being clear with God as to what your intention is.

Really getting a clear moment of thought, then you have to get out of the way... You have to stop planning, stop figuring it out, stop crunching numbers or deciding what your next move will be.

You must have faith, sit back and watch it unfold. From here you just watch and you see the door open up that you are meant to go through.

This will look mysterious because I guarantee 99.9% of the time it will come about in a way you would not have imagined because we don't see the whole picture... our minds are only able to see a tiny, tiny fraction of what's going on.

It's only when we quiet our minds and feel the great capacity of God (The All) that we shut up and realize we don't have all the answers.

We surrender our ego...

You have been clear, with God, as to what your intention is. Now it is being fulfilled just step out of the way and allow, allow, allow life to be different. Most of the time it will be unfamiliar to you because our thoughts are very narrow. If you don't allow life to be different God cannot fulfill your request.

The direction you will be led may not and most often will not look like anything you imagined.

I did not foresee going on the Camino and coming back feeling as if I had been downloaded with information to talk about of all things... God. If you had told me I was going to write about people's connection with the All I would have laughed in your face.

In my mind, I thought, "I love travel maybe I can write about travel"... but this? Nah!

I didn't even know I was going to walk the Camino until a couple months before we left.

I prayed for more direction and purpose in life and handed it over to God. This was the result and every day I have to get out of my own way to continue on this journey that I could not and would not have seen coming.

This is why the phrase "for the highest and best good of all involved" has been a go to for me, because it helps me center myself and imagine a win-win-win situation for everyone. The real kicker with all of this is getting your ego out of the way when the answer does come.

Use for example my sister Rose watching our dogs and the motor home while we were gone. I kept praying and "seeing as perfect" the end result. Everyone safe and happy and having gone through whatever spiritual lessons God had in store.

If it had been left up to me, and my decision making process, I would have never chosen to have her live in the motor home. She would have stayed living where she was, in a stagnate relationship, the dogs would have stayed with her, and the motor home would have been stored. That scenario made my ego feel safe...

But I prayed and I handed it (kicking and screaming) over to God. The result was better than I could have ever imagined.

Looking back I can see how she was able to grow more as a result of having been independent enough to conquer the RV... She was able to (emotionally) repay a debt, she felt she owed us, by loving something (our dogs) that she knows are so important to us, and she was able to step away from a relationship which had stalled.

Can you feel the energetic difference between these two scenarios? The spiritual growth of what ended up happening, for all of us, is so much more profound and important than my stupid "figured it out" plan. There was no growth potential in my scenario at all...

And this is just the part we can see... how much more is going on, on levels, we can't even comprehend?

Yet how many times do we make the decision to stay "safe"? Stay with what we know instead of allowing ourselves to be different and take the path that leads to our spirit's evolution.

If you feel like a fly banging your head against a glass window, it's probably because you are. Left to its own devices our minds can only continue to make the same decisions over and over again.

The fly on the window... bang... bang... bang.

Is it time to quiet your mind and allow life to be different than what you think it should be?

This question has helped me calm my mind for years; "Can you <u>let go of being so smart</u> and <u>allow it to be something other than you think it is</u>?" Ask yourself this whenever you feel frustrated, scared, holier than though, stuck, when something seems impossible. Ask yourself this several times a day and you will let go of the *stranglehold you have on your life needing to be just so... You will allow life to be different.*

We have to stop needing to be right in order for things to change and the fastest way to do this is to know and feel that you are safe in God's hands always. To have faith... Right or wrong, up or down, you are eternally safe and blessed and your mind is not what gives you that safety. In fact it hides the fact that you already are.... Safe, secure, loved and perfect. You already are perfect. Allow it to be so.

And maybe try this out for size.... God does not work in mysterious ways he just has the whole story. Continue to have faith!

Day 17 Carrion to Los Templarios

Cheers! We're 246 miles (397k) into the Camino Francés... Can somebody get me a taxi? This is a picture of us toasting our half way point at the end of our day...

Seriously my right leg hurts a lot! Tony carried my pack the last 5 miles again today... which makes me feel horrible!!! I've never had this injury so it's unfamiliar and I've never had to keep going day after day. Doing the same thing that caused the

pain in the first place, so that's odd. It's like cutting yourself in the morning, taking pains in the afternoon to ice it, take care of it, only to cut yourself again the next morning, hmmm.

I'm working on it physically and mentally trying to let the story go. There was a lot of anxiety leading up to this trip and in the first couple weeks so I know I have not been as peaceful as I should be.

Last night I lit a candle and prayed for help in being all loving (mine is the one tilting to the right in the middle) and this morning I could really feel the prayer being answered and for me the pain was a necessary part of it.

It calms me down, forces me to slow down, and I had the realization; even though I thought I was not walking fast, I had been. There was still pride and arrogance behind it. It was hidden there and it wasn't until I was humbled, to a crawl, this morning that I was able to see it. So the pain serves a purpose. I'm just afraid of where it goes from here.

I plan to send my pack ahead tomorrow so there's no chance Tony will have to carry it. Other than that all I can do is ice, rest, Fab 5, and hope...

We have our reservations made for tomorrow, which is nice, because it's beginning to get busier out here and accommodations are starting to get booked before we get into town.

The landscape today was (let's just say it) "ugly"... well at least to Tony and me it was anyway because it was very familiar. If you've ever been in central California you can Imagine walking down the 5 or 99 fwy in the Fresno/Bakersfield area. That's what it looked like today.

I was looking for a Del Taco. God I would kill for a burrito right now. We were trying to imagine ways to make chips and salsa without cilantro, jalapenos, chips... we gave up.

I took very few pictures today. Here is one direction

Here is the other...

Look who was back... My friend the poppy!

There was a town, right before the end today, Ledigos... We were laughing that is sounds like "let it go"...I'm trying... I'm trying!

That's it for today... Here's a fun picture from a communal dinner we were at, a couple nights ago, with our friends from Holland.

Ok better pics tomorrow... I promise!

Happy Friday!

Buen Camino

Lesson from the Camino... Gifts and Disappointments

Los Templarios is when I began to lose faith in the Guide books...

That's not really fair to say because the guidebooks hadn't done anything wrong it was my overinflated expectations which caused the problem.

Even though I was in pain I wanted to walk into town and see the Knights Templar Church. I had been looking forward to this town, and this moment, since we started the trip.

I couldn't though. I was in too much pain to make the one kilometer trek so I stayed put with my leg, iced and elevated, like a good girl. Then one of our "Camino friends" (the name I give for friends you make on the Camino and see over and over again even though you walk at completely different paces) came back from town and I asked if he had seen the Knights Templar Church? He said "What Church?" and I said "the guide books refer to this being one of the spots on the Camino where you can see a Knights Templar Church." and he said "No I don't think so, there's nothing in that town... I mean nothing."

"What?!" So I opened the guide book and re-read the page for about the one hundredth time. This time with new information, and new eyes, I saw it... "Terradillos de los Templarios was once home to a 13th Century church belonging to the Knights Templar"... <u>ONCE</u>

<u>I was pissed!</u>

How in the heck did I miss that? Now it was clear as day, and impossible to read otherwise, but because I was excited about it and my expectations didn't get met, because I had been hanging my hat on something outside of me to bring me joy, I was unable to see what was now so obvious. There was no church ... there used to be a church.

This happened to me over and over again on the Camino. I would get my hopes up about something, I read in the guide book, get there and be deeply disappointed.

- The roosters in Santo Domingo's Cathedral
- The Irache wine fountain
- This, my imagined, Knights Templar Church in Templarios
- The real Knights Templar Castle in Ponferrada (I say real because although there is one a castle in Ponferrada it's about as real as Sleeping Beauty's Castle in Disneyland... Beautiful but definitely contemporary)
- The Roman Road (just outside of Reliegos)
- The "Tree of Jesse" (not allowed to touch it anymore and at the time we were there behind a wall of construction so that you couldn't even see it!)

I did this to myself over and over again until I realized what I was doing. I was looking forward to preconceived events instead of letting the Camino surprise me.

Without fail every single thing I "looked forward to" was dismantled and yet every day the Camino had a special, unique, treasure just for me;

- The Poppies
- The thunderstorm in the monastery in Najera
- The elderly gentlemen, on their morning walks, (impeccably dressed) wishing us a "Buen Camino".
- The animals right alongside our path
- The majesty of the Pyrenees

Every day there was a special moment... a unique gift, to me, and it was in this town that I finally got it. Put down the book. Stop trying to figure out what's coming next and what you should be looking forward to. The Camino isn't about the obvious... the Camino has special things just for you.

Shut up and quit trying to figure it out... just sit back and watch.

Let it be... ALLOW those gifts to come into your life. If you're so wrapped up in what you think you're supposed to be looking forward to you're missing all the gifts along the way.

And they were beautiful!

Life has special gifts just for you... It won't be what you expect... remain open to seeing them because they are so much better than the guide books tell you.

Day 18 Sahagun and Angels on the Camino

Well last night was a doozy... My stomach hasn't been feeling well for several days but last night, after dinner, all hell broke loose... literally!

Sorry if this is TMI (too much information) but I promised to be honest with you all and truly blog the journey so here goes... I had explosive diarrhea all night. I couldn't even take a sip of water without having to run to the restroom. Add that to an all ready hurting leg and my tipping point had been met.

When the alarm went off this morning I told James and Tony there was no way I was walking today. I was taking a cab to Sahagun and getting anti-diarrheal medication. When I dosed in out and out of sleep I kept thinking I needed to go to Sahagun and in my dreams I kept spelling the name of the city to myself. S-A-H-A-G-U-N over and over again... It was being made extremely clear I needed to get to Sahagun.

Why? I had no idea.

Tony of course was not going to let me go alone and suggested we take a cab to our end destination, for the day, and seek help there but I listened to my dream and said "No I don't know why but I need to go to Sahagun".

James headed out for his day and we hung back and tried to rest until we knew stores would be open.

Today has been a day of angels... My husband first of all... God I married a good man! Those of you who know him know it's true but he is so sweet. He didn't skip a beat in giving up the walk and taking care of me. I am so blessed. Then every where we went we needed help. We had to ask the man at our albergue to call us a taxi. (Talking on the phone when you don't speak the language is nearly impossible) Several times today we had to go into albergues and ask them to call someone for us. These people aren't getting paid to do this... They will never see us again and we aren't even guests of their establishments but they do it anyway. That's very kind.

We got a cab to Sahagun and asked him to take us to a farmacia. We found one that was open and then had to do charades to explain diarrhea and needing it to stop! He spoke no English but got it... and handed me the correct pills but then trying to figure out the dosage, he was telling me to take, was a little tricky. I thought he said "two every two hours" and Tony thought he said "one" so we went with the lower dosage.

That stuff works amazingly fast so I was okay after that. Just weak.

Then we bopped into another albergue and pointed to our feet demonstrating a massage and he gave us a card and showed us a place on the map.

We walked over to what I thought was going to be a reflexology/ foot massage centre so we could both get a much needed break but it ended up being a Doctor's office of a whole lot of things we couldn't read on his walls. He was very nice and welcoming and told us he could help and to come by at 11.

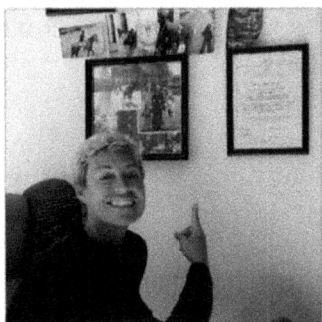

We went to a cafe, had an orange juice (close to a potty in case the medicine hadn't kicked in yet) and waited.

A little before 11 we went and sat in his lobby at Centros de Masaje

The Doctor called us in and I showed him my swollen ankle and shin and he said it's one of the most common injuries on the trail.

He then proceeded to unleash a myriad of treatments first massage, not gentle but not too hard either, just right. He was very caring and proceeded to read me the riot act while treating me. "All pain is psychosomatic" he said. "You have problems on your right side which is your masculine side. Who are you having issues with, your father?"

He searched for male figures but of course, not knowing me, he could only search but I knew without a doubt... I was angry and I hadn't let it go and now here it was in physical manifestation. A physical manifestation of my failure to be at Peace. I felt deeply ashamed.

Dr. David went on...
"You aren't drinking enough water. You need to eat more fruit for the magnesium and potassium. You need to stop drinking coffee" and although he didn't specifically say alcohol he said to absolutely stay away from sugar. Which I do... but alcohol is sugar too... which I have not stayed away from.

Let's face it I got my hand slapped for everything I know better than but haven't been doing.

This morning lying in bed, feeling miserable, I couldn't fathom staying here for 18 more days. I pictured getting on a train in Leon and a plane within a couple days. But I knew I had a choice I could either take this as an opportunity to clean up my act and become a different person by the end, of this, or I could run home having had a beautiful vacation but no change.

Dr. David then started telling us about the Camino and how important this portion, Sahagun, is to the journey. He said I should visit the monastery there and meditate. He reiterated the story of the different sections of the Camino; Life, Death and Rebirth. He said the section from Burgos to Leon is the death section where we really have to go inside, become quiet and internalize. Well I guess I purged myself good on this one!

He then proceeded to do Chiropractic, Acupuncture and Energy work, on me, and Tony and I, started to piece together what all the degrees were on the walls.
For those back home Imagine my sister Laura (an amazing massage therapist), Dr. Mike Andrews and Dr. Jeremiah Cheratt (A.R.T. experts and Chiropractors) put together with an acupuncturist, and a faith healer and you've met Dr. David.

I was floored by how thorough he was and I was glad I had a background with everything he was doing. I can only imagine what someone who has never had these things done to them would have thought...

But I was so blessed to have found him. Here's his website in case you are in need of help in Leon or Sahagun. He is truly amazing! www.masajescaminodesantiago.com

We left his office and asked another albergue to help us call a taxi, which they did... and Yvonne showed up to take us to our place for the night. She was a doll!

It was so weird to be in a taxi. Today was our first car ride in 18 days, and to whiz by all the peregrinos on the Camino. Very surreal seeing it from the other side.

Here's the monastery in Sahagun

And us whizzing by everything in the taxi Bittersweet but necessary... Don't know what's going to happen tomorrow... but there were a lot of angels today :-) and I feel very blessed.

Tony is doing great no issues for him... as he says "I walk light" meaning he walks with a happy heart and very little stress and it shows.

I'm learning, I'm learning :-)

Lesson from the Camino... It doesn't matter who you think you are

About a week after we got home, it was raining outside (a rarity for Southern California) so we didn't have much to do and we decided it would be fun to spend the afternoon re-watching two of the movies we had watched before leaving to Spain.

One was a documentary called; Six Ways of the Camino

And the other was "The Way" which we had seen several times.

We thought it would be fun to watch them from the vantage point of having been there. (On a side note, before we left I remember saying, in reference to Six ways of the Camino, "Wow if it's that beautiful I'm going to love it there"... It was far more beautiful than even the movie captures.)

So we sat down and watched the documentary first... 40 minutes into the movie we both gasped. There on the screen was the very Doctor "Dr. David" we had seen in Sahagun...W.T.F.!!!!

We rewound it because his part is very small and we had to make sure we had just seen the same thing. There he was, the man that was so kind to me, in Sahagun, and had seen us with no appointment. Who just happened to be in his office when we came by and just happened to have an opening within the hour.

Here's the deal; I went to his office because I was looking for a reflexology massage. I was just hoping Tony and I could both have our feet worked on and he came out and was so warm and friendly. Normally I would not have stayed because I didn't want a lot of attention and a big process with a Doctor... I just wanted a massage.

If he had said we had to wait until the afternoon or to come back, even an hour later, I wouldn't have (you know that patience thing). I would have felt like I was making too big of a deal out of all this and I could just let some time pass and "get over it".

But he didn't... he was with a client and he said to "come back in 20 minutes" and so we did. Had I, and my ego mind, had anything to do with it... I would have never made this appointment.

God had other things in mind.

Dr David is very special. I consider myself blessed to have met him. He has a deep connection with the Camino and in a very kind way... He'll let you have it and then he'll help you heal.

I lay on that table while he told me everything I already knew.

The first words out of his mouth were "all problems are psychosomatic" Which Tony and I firmly believe. All physical issues begin first as thoughts and energy.

Everything is first energy.

These imbalanced thoughts then manifest themselves in the physical as disease, injury, pain, etc throughout the body.

The fact of the matter is I was out of balance and I knew it. I had been out of balance since Day 1 of the Camino and it had finally reached a head, and boiling point, in Burgos and into Los Templerios.

I had warning signs... I knew I was carrying anger and I was struggling to release the anger and return to the

Peace. I knew I was failing at accomplishing the task on my own.

I knew I was eating like shit and I saw more warning signs that speak to me personally (several dead frogs). A sign to me that a physical cleanse is necessary and imminent. When I see this I know if I don't do it, Mother Nature is going to do it for me, in the form of me getting sick and I better clean up my act.

I lay on Dr. David's table as he continued to tell me all the things I already knew...

"You shouldn't be drinking coffee"..."Alcohol"

"You aren't eating enough fruit"... "You need to eat apricots and figs for the magnesium and potassium"

I'm thinking "You have no idea who I am. This is what I freaking do for a living. I tell people how to eat!". Well you know what?... It doesn't matter who the F I think I am... The fact of the matter is I'm the idiot laying on this table sick as a dog!!!! What I know is irrelevant if I'm not going to do it...."

"So shut the F up and listen to this guy."

And so I did...

Lesson --- It doesn't matter who you are or what you know... If you aren't doing it someone's going to remind you. Thank you Dr. David you are a wonderful man and we are blessed to have met you.

If you are in Sahagun, or Leon, and you get the opportunity to make an appointment and visit him, you should, he is truly a gift of the Camino.

Day 19 We're still kickin... Calzadilla de los Hermanillos to Mansilla de las Mulas

Just checking in, quickly, with everyone to tell you all is well. We spent last night in Casa El Cura. A referral from our friends at the Chill Cafe. Staying there took us off the "main" Camino for a moment and onto an alternate path.

It was a great place and the proprietors were a REAL treat! So nice, so fun, and the homemade food was very good. It was just what I needed. I pulled the covers over my head and slept, all day, after seeing Dr. David and taking the cab to Calzadilla. I got out of bed only to eat their home made meal and crawl back into bed.

But today I'm doing so much better! Not a lot of pictures today only because there wasn't a lot to take pictures of. We are very much looking forward to hitting Leon tomorrow and getting off the Meseta.

I was able to walk most of the way today, with my pack, but then Tony had to take it again at the end. A little more rest tomorrow and I should be right as rain.

Here's some of the Camino today... We had the excitement of

switching from pavement to dirt road at one point but it was pretty much a straight, flat, shot all the way.

and this is a Roman road they have left covered in dirt and fenced off but you can pretend you can see it like we did... (Yes I was looking forward to it the whole day... No I haven't learned yet)

We took a break, from the sun, under a few different trees today. Tony was very happy because I agreed to sit down and take a break and they were beautiful. As I looked up they reminded me of our family's yard in Northern California and sitting under their big tree with our doggies... Sigh.

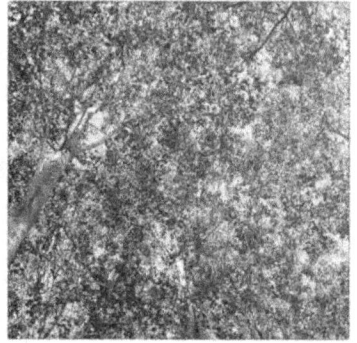

Love ya'll Happy Father's Day!

Day 20 The vibrancy is coming back... Mansilla de las Mulas to Leon

I can see a light at the end of this Meseta tunnel and it's called Leon! A visit to Leon's beautiful Gothic Cathedral this morning boosted our energy. You could literally feel a buzz and according to Dr. David there is a buzz... He told us to go to the inside of the Catedral (Cathedral), walk to the center, take a necklace and hold it out, like a pendulum, and the necklace would spin, on its own.

He said this is due to the energy vortex in the center of the massive cathedral and it totally did!

He says the center of the Cathedral is the strongest point of energy on the Camino.

We used my Camino necklace and it even spun in the opposite direction we expected, so it wasn't us doing it.

No matter how many times we tried, it spun counter clockwise... weird!

I felt a little woozy coming out of there but that was, most likely, because of trying to do back bends, to get pictures of the stained glass in the incredibly high ceilings, than anything else.

The only thing I really wish is there was a stair case which allowed you to see the stained glass up closer. It's so beautiful but so far away.

My stomach is 100% better and my leg is 50% just needs time to heal.

Unfortunately walking every day does not allow for that so we have a new best friend Lazaro. He's our taxi driver. I'll try and get a picture of him tomorrow but he's been skipping us ahead a bit so I can keep the distances short.

We didn't intend it that way but we called him once to take 4 miles off a day, and he was so sweet, we called him again this morning to take us into Leon and now we've called him for tomorrow to help shorten the walk up tomorrow... fingers crossed, by then, it'll be 100%.

Plus after that point we'll be too far away for Lazaro to come get us so it'll have to be better! It has no choice.... "Do you hear that leg?".... "No more Lazaro!"

We knew today, being in a big city, we would have the opportunity to find a Mc Donald's... not only did we find one we also found something I have been craving like a fiend... Chips and Salsa!!!!!

We found them in this iconic American novelty shop... that's how rare chips and salsa are. The only place you can find them is a novelty shop. How crazy is that?

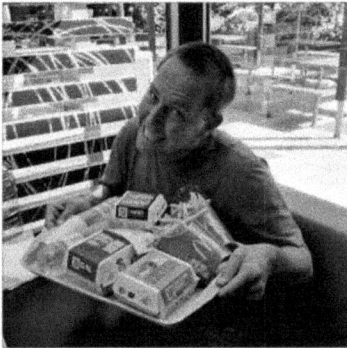

Yes even Tony ate Mc Donalds. Trust me I know this from past experience you will never appreciate a Big Mac more than when you're in a foreign Country. Then it tastes amazing!!!

We were trying to think of the last time we ate at a Micky D's and we think it's about 5 years ago when we did Mt. Whitney... and it tasted good too!
We're celebrating big time tonight.

This is a big benchmark for James. Including the mileage of his PCT (pacific crest trail) excursion he has now crossed 500 miles in 3 months... Wow!

To celebrate we are staying in the famous San Marcos Parador highlighted in the movie *The Way* with Martin Sheen.

The room <u>isn't</u> spectacular but being inside the building is awesome enough!!!

Here we also say goodbye to James for a little while. He won't be skipping ahead, as we will, so it may be a little bit before we see him again but the Camino always has tricks in store.

Love ya'll Adios until next time....

Day 21 Leon to Astorga (with taxi service from Leon to Hospital de Orbigo)

I walked the whole way, from Hospital de Orbigo to Astorga, without giving Tony my pack today!!!! Okay so it was only 18 k (11 miles) but it's the most I've done with my pack on, in a few days, so I'm stoked! I'm posting the blog late today because the town we're in, Astorga, is awesome! We had so much to see once we got to town.

Now here's the problem not only do you have to be fit enough to get to the towns but then sometimes you want to be able to walk around and just be a tourist for a little while and Astorga is one of those places. Here you really want to save some reserve energy or plan on spending an extra day because this place is Cute!

In the 18th and 19th centuries Astorga was known for it's chocolate production. Yum.. although I will say the chocolate museum was a bit of a bust.... But we got samples at the end YAY!

There were several highlights today, besides the walk, (which was back to being quite pretty) but I have to say the number #1 highlight of the day was the Spa in our hotel, Ciudad de Astorga.

We had the entire place to ourselves. You go around the pool pushing different buttons and the jets do all these crazy things at each station. It was a BLAST... literally.

My absolute favorite was a full body shower (you can see the stall behind Tony in the picture) which you could section off to different areas of the body, for example your calves, and the water would alternate between very hot and very cold. It was amazing!

The blast lasts about a minute and I must have gone in that shower 20 times at a minimum. Then there was a sauna, a steam room, jacuzzi and a pool at the perfect temperature. I was in heaven and we felt so relaxed when we left there our feet were like "thank you, thank you, thank you" . Can you say prune?

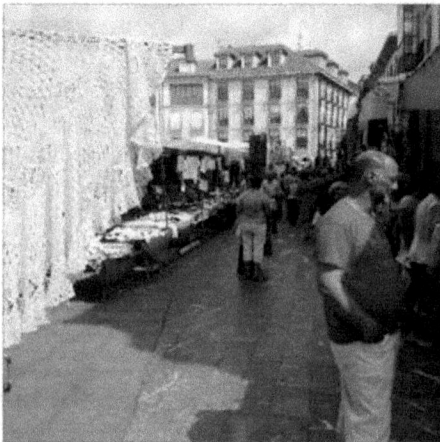

This spa was my Camino gift of the day. It was exactly what we needed! Thank you Camino! Astorga is a busy little city and the farmers market beat all the others we've seen by far. It winds through several streets and a large square and has everything you don't need.

The walk was much prettier today...

and this guy was an interesting dude. He seems to live here on the Camino and gives food out from his garden for donation only...

Very peaceful place.

Great vibes!

Here are some more pics from the trail today...

and here is one of our Camino Angels, our taxi driver Lazaro, who took us to our starting point this morning. He was such a genuinely sweet person we will miss Lazaro but glad we don't need him.

We had him take us to Hospital de Orbigo this morning so we could skip some city walking and shorten our trek up today. The funny part is we had him drop us off at a bridge, Rio Orbigo, which is a famous bridge on the Camino.

He left us on the side of the road and drove off and we were standing in the middle of basically a freeway.

We looked at each other and thought. "Uh Oh this doesn't look right!" We walked about 100 yards and no arrows.

We pulled out our guide books and tried to figure out what happened. Till I realized "uh oh" there would be several bridges that cross this river not necessarily the correct bridge. And we could see on the map that the major highway he dropped us off on would, in fact, take us to Astorga but it was not the "recommended" route for the

Camino. You see many times there are several Caminos at once. Popular routes and not so popular routes, greener, harder to find routes and more urban routes. A lot of times you are choosing your Camino.

So he had dropped us off on a road that would take us to Astorga but we wanted our arrows back! Do you remember in early grade school when you went on a field trip and they would make you all hold hands and create a long chain or you would all have to hold onto a rope so you wouldn't get lost?

Well the Camino arrows, no matter how silly they seem at times, become like a giant rope to hold onto and it isn't until those arrows are gone that you freak out and realize you really want your arrows back!!!

So after only a couple minutes of panic we found our arrows and the correct river crossing Which in this case is an iconic Gothic bridge known for a Knight who jousted 300 knights and beat every one in order to heal his lovesick heart. The bridge is seen below and it is magnificent! I'm so glad we found it!

And I'm so glad we didn't walk to Astorga on a major highway... Yuck!

(Incidentally Hospital de Orbigo is an adorable town and I am sad we didn't get to spend more time there as well.)

Ultreia until tomorrow...

Pre-day 22 Lesson from the Camino... Rocks

Before we left for the Camino I asked some of our friends, back home, if they would like me to take a rock, for them, to the Cruz Ferro.

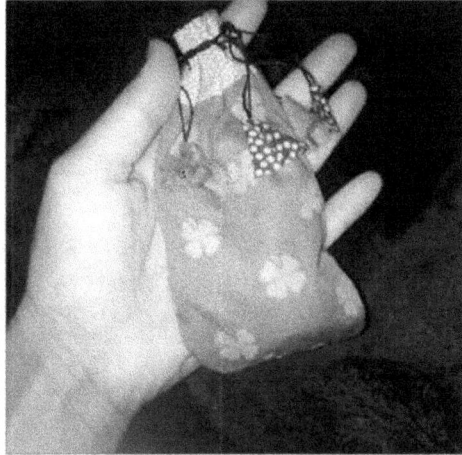

The Cruz de Ferro is a cross marking the highest point on the Camino and it is customary to leave a rock here asking for forgiveness for something or as John Brierley so beautifully puts it in his guide book "add your token of love and blessing to the great pile that witnesses to our collective journeying."

A few of our friends took us up on the offer and this post was in regards to carrying those rocks....

We're only a couple days away from the Cruz de Ferro. You may be surprised to learn more than a few times these rocks, your rocks, have helped to motivate me to get this far. "I have to get their rocks there. I have to keep going". So thank you for that...

When I lay my rock down at the Cruz Ferro, I will be asking for forgiveness and freedom from my ego. And in true "ego" fashion my initial thought was "It'll have to be a boulder, so large, I won't be able to carry it" but see that's the funny thing about ego...

It wants you to believe it's huge and insurmountable but in truth it's tiny and insignificant and as I have learned over the past couple years, relatively easy to free yourself of.

I have spent the last few years learning to meditate and release the ego portion of my mind and once I experienced the bliss and peace of that you never want to go back.

When you have the courage to stop listening to your ego a whole new world opens up. it takes practice and it doesn't stay gone for long. It will always be there, or at least I haven't been able to rid myself of it completely, maybe with the help of this rock... but at least understanding how the computer works has given me so much peace.

I am so much happier now than I was a few years ago and nothing in my life has changed except this piece of the puzzle... I didn't have to make more money, or move, or buy x, y or z. I just learned to stop my amygdala from running the show and that is a gift I wish everyone could experience.

Which is why I now teach what I have learned because it was a gift given to me and I am so thankful to have received it I would never withhold it from anyone.

Imagine something in life you love... something that when you look at it you have no judgment whether it be something in nature like the ocean, or a puppy, or new born baby, a flower as it blooms, a leaf as it falls from a tree?

Take a moment and experience what that feeling feels like in your heart and how your mind quiets for a moment. There's no judgment... even if it's not perfect you still see the perfection in the imperfection. Now imagine feeling that way about and towards everything in life.

PairOfGringos.com

That's a glimpse at peace. The dropping of the need to judge, the need for the ego mind to protect us.

Our minds are nothing more than computers and the ego is simply a piece of the mind.... a function of that computer. Left to its own devices it simply runs the same pre-set programs over and over and over again. It's only when you learn to ignore that tiny piece and override that function of the computer, you begin to pull back the curtain on what you really are. The eternal bliss... and you see it's all been one big joke. We run around like crazy people trying to protect ourselves from every threat, every moment of the day, when it was just a tiny "animalistic" portion of our brains running the show. All that worry completely unnecessary.

Imagine what you would have time to do and experience without worry. If you truly knew you were always safe and loved? How would you be different?

On the Camino you become hyper-aware because everything is new and your mind is on high alert. This brings out the worst in people's egos. It's been both sad and interesting to watch. You meet someone new and they lead with their ego... We all do it but for those who haven't recognized how to subdue their reactive tendencies they never get out of it. Constantly either seeking approval "what can I do to get this person to like me" or putting up their guard to avoid being hurt... or needing to control the situation.

If you watch you'll see this in pretty much every encounter, in every day life, as well but here it's heightened because every one is new and everything happening around the person is new.
So you see a bunch of ping pong balls, pinging off each other, trying to appease their egos and as long as that's

what's running the show... trust me you never get anywhere. It's an endless loop

I see ego everywhere here, even in the churches. They admit themselves the churches were a form of competition, from village to village, to see who could create the highest arches, the most stained glass, the most gold on the altar.

When you pull back the great curtain of oz you see everything

And so although the churches are beautiful, works of art, and sometimes you are in awe that you are standing in a building whose foot print is a thousand years old. I have to admit it I still prefer to go outside...

Because if I go outside, drop to my knees and pick up a rock I'm holding something that God made, not man, and now you have my attention.

So at the Cruz de Ferro I will pick up a rock, drop to my knees and first say thank you for the peace I have already received and then in true "ego" fashion ask for more... Freedom from the ego, to peer into the magnitude of what we truly are. Already perfect, already beautiful, already eternally loved.

Amen and Thank you Lord

Day 22 Astorga to Rabanal del Camino

I love going uphill so today was my kind of day. A slow and steady climb up out of Astorga 13 miles (20.6k) into Rabanal del Camino and Tony didn't have to carry my pack today... woo hoo! No Tony Camel...

We opted to not push our luck today and stayed in Rabanal instead of pushing on another 3 miles (6k) to Foncebadon. Plus as we came through Rabanal del Camino it was such a cute town we couldn't resist staying.

I guess that means no scary, wild dog, ghost stories for us tonight. Apparently Paolo Coelho in his book, *The Pilgrimage*, and Shirley Maclaine's *The Camino* both describe encounters with wild, vicious dogs in Foncebadon so hopefully we'll be skipping that and we'll dream of puppies and kittens instead.

Here are some of the sights as we left Astorga this morning...

A few miles outside of Astorga, we had breakfast at a cute little place and the owner was a riot... Half sweet, half fiery. Her place was packed and the food was good but she was yelling at everybody.

While I was waiting in line somebody got yelled at for touching the fruit (not us this time... we're learning) "Don't touch my fruit" she screamed and someone else got yelled at for leaving the lights on, in the bathroom, "You must be rich where you live. Here electricity is expensive!". Then she would go back to smiling, laughing, kissing people and making the food. What a character! I had a fresh pressed juice with carrots, oranges and ginger... Yipes flavorful! and A huge sandwich and Tony had Muesli with rice milk. He was so excited to see she had rice milk!

Then we started our slow climb...

Today the scenery changed dramatically as we went... First we had shrubs and almost desert like conditions.

It felt a little like Sedona, Az. Then we entered Santa Catalina...

Here I wanted to show you show you how cute some of the Albergues are in these little towns...

As Tony says "you can never tell what it's going to look like on the inside from the front" and you really can't.

You can be looking at the most boring exterior and you open the door into an amazing garden or something crazy.

and here are a few cyclists whizzing through!

Then it was off to El Ganso ,very quiet, not much going on but this cute little place, The Cowboy Bar.

Once we left El Ganso we got some trees back..

As we started to climb into a beautiful forest...

As you near Rabanal you begin to see an expansive wire fence, Via Crucis. This is where many Pilgrims have placed sticks to create about a bazillion wooden crosses... Yes I counted it was exactly a bazillion...

We found the "Holland couple" sitting resting here and sat down and had a nice visit with them before entering Rabanal.

When we arrived in Rabanal del Camino there was a Falcon waiting for us... Cool!
Our room for the night is great! El Tesin..

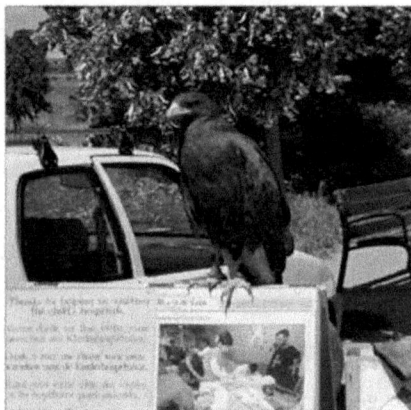

Very Nice owners, good food, cute place...

Very much looking forward to tomorrow...

It's Rock time at Cruz Ferro!!! and then on to a Knight's Templar Castle if we decide to push all the way through to Ponferrada.

Ultreia!

Day 23 The Package has been Delivered!
Rabanal del Camino to Acebo

We stepped over the 300 mile mark today!

We're at mile marker 345 miles of the Camino (555 K) so take 345 minus 40 miles of taxi service and that's 305 miles all on foot.... 305 divided by 23 is 13.25 miles per day... so a half marathon every day for 23 days...

Kind of funny to think of it that way.

But as I keep reminding myself this is not a race! For me it's not even an athletic event. This is touring a country, we just happen to be doing most of the touring on foot.

I have done enough athletic events in my life. This needs to be something different and I am learning to walk slower (partially thanks to the injury).

I am learning to notice, in myself, that I was still falling into the habit of competing with people up a hill. Seeing which men I could pass. This is not what my journey is about and that needed to stop.

I am thankful I noticed it and saw the pride and arrogance behind it, even though it was subtle, it was still there.

Now when I'm about to pass someone I make sure my energy is clear before I do it. If there is any pride I stop and slow down until I've let go of the thought and am only loving.

Speaking of pain 17 k (apx 11 miles) today of (virtually) pain free walking... Yay! As long as I walk cautiously, and deliberately, I feel almost no pain. I was thinking this morning how if I were at home I would be doing Fab 5, Joint rotations, taking the dogs on an easy 2-3 mile dog walk (with a cup of coffee in my hand), maybe some upper body work but the absolute last thing I would be doing, on this leg, is walking 11 miles!!!!

But the body is amazing and it's healing abilities remarkable! it's doing great despite not being able to lay off it... Super thrilled with that! Thank you Fab 5 and Dr. David for that extra push!

Today was beautiful! Please visit our blog to see all the Pics because we can't get them all in here and we don't want you to miss the beauty! www.PairofGringos.com

... lots of up! In fact today we reached one of the *highest point on the Camino 1500m (4921 ft) which is marked by the Cruz de Ferro.

And we got to drop off the rocks!!! Woo HOOOOO!!!! Thanks again for letting us carry them. It really does feel like many of you are along for the ride, with us, both in allowing us to carry your rocks and in following the blog and it really has motivated us to keep going through some of the more boring or painful days.

Here are the rocks... and a last minute entry :-) I got an email from home last night with a friend asking me to add one more rock to the pile... Happy to do it!

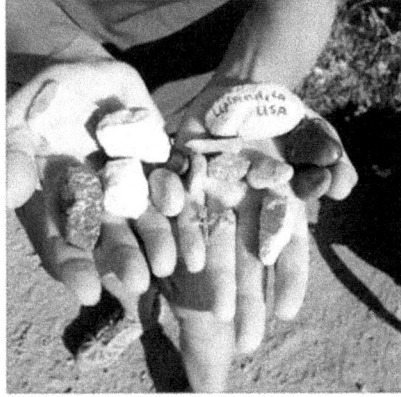

and mine... letting go of the dark (ego) into the light (I kept the light one)

There was an empty circle up there just for us (they must periodically come through and clear it because I can't believe there was an empty spot like that... our rocks fit perfectly!) And yes I felt lighter immediately!

So the package has been delivered... hope you could feel a lightening of spirit or at least a part of the journey whatever you had hoped for. It's been quite a trip.

Back to the day,...

Knock, knock "Hi Honey I'm home"

We climbed through some beautiful fern this morning...

Into Foncebadon... and the only "vicious" dogs we encountered were a couple adorable puppies!!

Then more climbing... Here's the view looking back over the valley we climbed out of.

And more great signs... The Graffiti on the Camino is awesome! So entertaining!

This one reads "Jeremy Keep the flame alive. See you at the end of the earth or the next one...

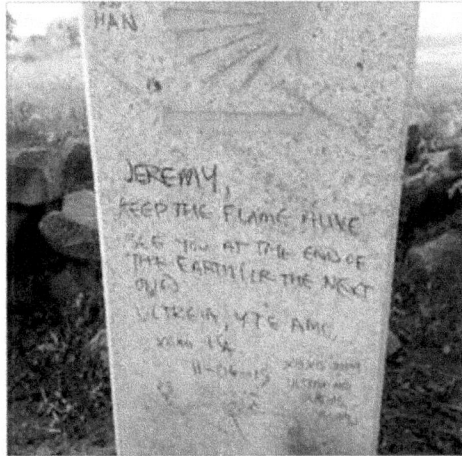

Ultreia!" Love that a note left to most likely someone they had to leave behind in that town.

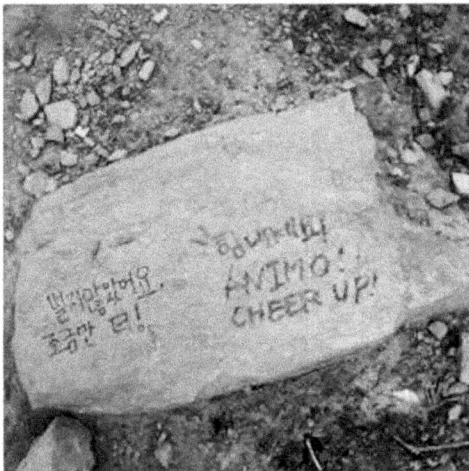

Claudia this one's for you... We've seen it written all over the trail but I didn't know what it meant until you mentioned it... Animo!

One at the base of a cross read... "We are pure energy" Love it!

Then there was this really bizarre place... apparently the owner considers himself the last modern day Templar. Right after him you reach the actual summit 1520 meters (4987ft No idea why the Cruz Ferro isn't there)

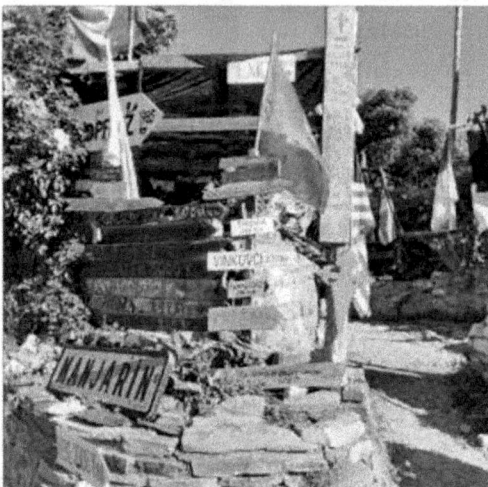

Later we had a nice respite at this mobile snack stand... Where we met a woman from Palm Springs (standing next to Tony in the pic below).

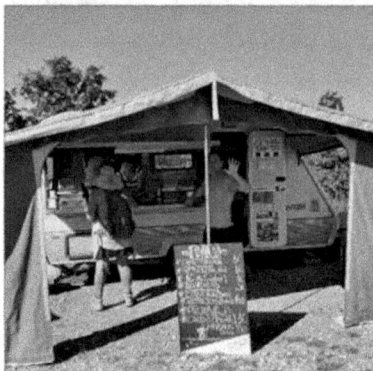

It's so funny when you meet someone from "home". You, instantly, have so much in common. The conversation went something like this (once we finished commiserating about the physical pain everyone experiences and talks about)

Her... "Can you believe all the bread?" Me... "NO! If I never see bread or Jamon again in my life I'll be perfectly fine with that." Her... "My gluten free friends at home would never believe this" Me... "My vegan sister would starve to death here." It's a pretty funny conversation.

We fell into an instant friendship she reminded me of all our boot campers scooped up into one.

Then down it was... Here you can see the valley you start to descend into. In the far off distance is, Ponferrada, a big city of about 69,000. We'll be there tomorrow...

Decided to cut it a little short today and ended up in Acebo because it's not a race and we are reminding ourselves with each step, and every moment, "to be here now"... "Enjoy the journey".

All day my mantra was "Be here now... be purposeful".

Something Tony and I have been working on for a few days now. It's so easy to get caught up in thinking about things other than where you are right at this moment. In the now and enjoying the present. We just kept looking up, stopping our thoughts from turning to the next mile, or the next town, or the next whatever, taking a deep breath and Being in the present. Raise your energy where you are now and things will change. You don't have to "try" or "figure things out" you just have to be clear where you are right now, raise your own energy and things come to you. The signs just appear when you are clear. So we decided to stop in this adorable town and enjoy the afternoon instead of pushing on.

Beautiful room, good food, friendly staff... at La Casa Del Peregrino and I don't think I've ever seen a black flower before... There's one, on the balcony, right outside our room.

Phew! lots of pics today... Happy Thursday... Enjoy your Now!

Lesson from the Camino... Responsibility

It was on the descent, into Acebo, that I felt a strong wave come over me. I was being impressed with a message that my prayers had been answered. I would be allowed to share what I had done here and help people find peace but that with it came a huge responsibility.

It was a powerful moment... one that I do not take lightly and will never forget.

I came home "knowing" to write this book and who knows where it goes from here but I know it's in God's hands and the "how" is not my job.

Day 24 Back up on the Horse... Acebo to Cacabelos

Today we woke up with a different attitude. The feeling was one of... "Okay now this is a job.

Let's get this done." (We'll see how long that lasts)... Which is strange because that was not the energy of the past couple days but we just go with the flow... so push we did.

We jammed 5 miles, down hill, to Molinesca. All pretty steep and the terrain was almost entirely rocks... yikes!

Here's me adding an "L" to Molinesca to spell my name...
Molinesca is a beautiful town and I am sad we missed this quaint city with it's inviting swimming hole, the night before, but I am glad we didn't do that major DOWNHILL 5 miles on tired legs.

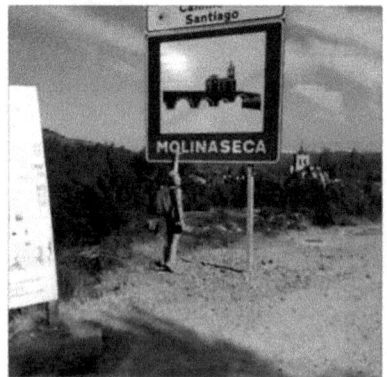

Down hill hurts on sore legs!

We took a lot of pictures today so please visit the blog because I hate to have you miss them! www.PairofGringos.com Day 24...

They like to do these decorative roads covered in rocks here... they may be pretty but boy do they hurt on tired peregrino feet!

We stepped aside and were entertained as watched cars and pedestrians passing each other on the narrow streets.

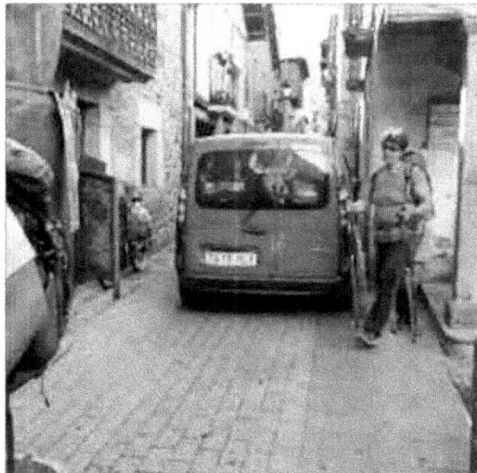

Then it was onto the large city of Ponferrada where I was insistent upon seeing the Knights Templar Castle (Castillo de los Templarios).

I thought we would just walk around the outside but when we got there it was open and so we toured it quickly.

When I say quickly I mean we ran through the place taking as many pictures as possible.

It's quite extensive. It was stunning but I was again very disappointed, because although the footprint is 12th century, it has been completely remodeled into this modern day castle. I was really hoping it would be a real castle but I guess that's not possible. It was beautiful nonetheless.

There were only a few scary bits... Please see the blog we took lots of pics!

Inside they have an extensive collection of Bibles (Bibliotecas) which we both found fascinating. They are of course copies as well... sigh... but it's a very important collection and there is no way they could

PairOfGringos.com

display the real thing in public like that, too precious and easily damaged so this is the closest any of us will ever come.

Then we had to hustle as it was a hot day and we had miles to go before we rest...

The Camino takes you through a city park along a river as you travel through Ponferrada. We watched a dog getting a drink from a fountain. It was so cute he walked (no leash) right up to the fountain and waited for his owner to get there and push the button for him... adorable!
The walk through the park turned into a not so pretty walk out of Ponferrada

Then I put the camera away... Too hot... had to get down to the business of walking.

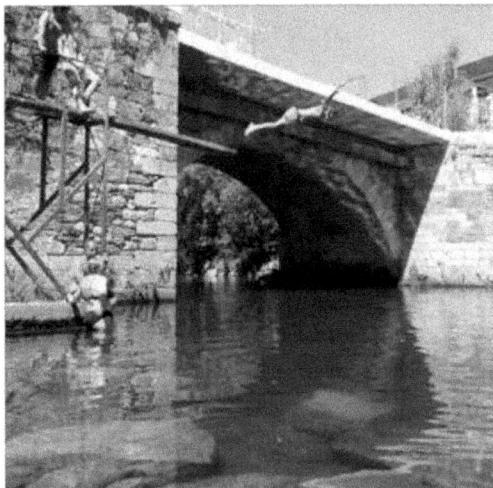

Imagine lots of vineyards... (We didn't even stop at the wine co-op as I said our energy had completely shifted in Acebos we went from taking it all in and purposely slowing down to 5th gear... get her done!

We got to Cacabelos and found a place for the night and everyone hanging out at this fun swimming hole... We stuck our feet in, too tired to put on our bathing suits, and celebrated our longest day in awhile 20 miles (apx 32k).

I wished we could have made it all the way to Villafranca del Bierzo because it's a beautiful town but all is good... no complaints... we don't need luxury every night and our hospitalero at El Molino is a great guy.

We'll see Villafranca tomorrow as we walk through.

Tomorrow starts another steep climb... woo hoo... I love mountains!!!

Ultreia!

Day 25 Today was 23 miles (37k) of Up...

I happen to really like hiking up mountains (and Tony's cool with whatever) so it was awesome, for us, but I can imagine this portion of the journey is really difficult for many, many people (I think a lot of people must cab this part).

I decided today's hike was the perfect bookend to the Pyrenees (anyone who knows what the first day's hike out of St. Jean Pied de Port is like now knows what I'm talking about as far as difficulty) They bookend each other beautifully. 25 days ago when we started the Camino Frances, St Jean, you do a crazy climb over the Pyrenees... You walk for many, many days and now it feels like you climb back out via this climb into O Cebreiro. Now it feels like all that's left is to slide into home.

The most common route for the day takes you from Villafranca del Bierzo to O Cebreiro which is 18 miles (29 k) but we started 5 miles further back and had to play catch up making our day 23 miles.

The first 20 miles were a gradual climb along a not too busy highway... (with a major freeway running overhead most of the way) and very little shade.

It was somewhere between 85-90 degrees (32 C) so it was HOT!

With the last 3 miles (5k) being some of the steepest climbs you can get!

We hit the hardest part around 3pm with the afternoon sun blaring down on us... (SUPER HOT) and all I could think is "We're okay. We are athletes and we know exactly how our body's are going to respond... but If I see anyone else out here doing this at this hour... they're IDIOTS!" Luckily we only saw a small group of male teenagers (who looked flabbergasted when we past them), one hiker who appeared to be more than competent and one young couple... We checked on them all as we passed and I saw them all make it to the top later so good deal... Turns out a 35 year old guy died on that spot last week... When I say it's no joke... I'm not kidding.

Sadly the vast majority of the people hiking the Camino are in way over the heads with the physicality of this challenge. We were talking to a couple from the Yukon, in Canada, a few days back and although they are relatively fit and do many outdoor sports. They were not prepared for how taxing the Camino has been.

They commented that they really felt the guidebooks did not properly warn them of what is required, physically, and I have to agree. Add to that they aren't used to the heat.

They were pretty much planning on bailing and going back to the Louvre in Paris. She was as pink as a lobster, with heat rash, and sunburn so I'm sure they won't be on the Camino much longer. Poor things, but they'll have a wonderful time in Paris...

Here are some pics... Here's me eating breakfast, of watermelon, on the run... literally!

We attempted to lighten the load as much as possible by ditching our last sleeping bag here... (We left it sitting on a chair outside a cafe). You could go into business here collecting all the stuff Pilgrim's leave behind!

Just after this bridge there is an alternate route some people choose to take. Taking the alternate route keeps you off of the main highway and in more of the forest.

We met a group of 3 men who had missed the turn off for the alternate route and had walked back in an attempt to find it. I pulled out both our guidebooks (we carried 2 different books) and one did clearly show the alternate route so we showed it to the men and they thanked us and went on their way.

If you are traveling with more than 1 person I do recommend taking different guidebooks. It's nice to get additional info at times...

The main Camino has you climbing next to a river most of the day....

If you like "climbing" on a bike I think this would be one of your favorite days, by far. It follows well paved highways, through beautiful mountains, but if you don't like climbing I would avoid it all together.

The last part of the climb into O'cebreiro is a popular area for renting horses to make the climb. Tony was tempted to try a horse ... but I explained all the reasons a horse would in fact not be fun and he agreed.

Leaving La Faba we started the steepest part of the climb on our own two feet... (Hmmm... maybe Tony's idea was better :-) Just kidding I loved this part but it was very tough and very hot! And only a tiny fraction of the hike is in the shade. Here's a picture looking back over the climb up...

Then you finally cross over into Galicia... Seafood here we come! We've heard the food is much better in this region and so far that has turned out to be true... Thank God!

So we made it through what should be the last really strenuous day... Leg is 100% now... woo hoo!

Ultreia until the end...!

P.s. I've had to turn my phone off (which is also my camera) the last couple days so the pictures became less than spectacular and much less frequent. Also as I mentioned our attitude has switched from one of "slow down and enjoy the journey" to "This is a job let's get er' done!" which makes picture taking a little less of a priority for us but there are still more pics on the blog for you to see!!! www.PairOfGringos.com

Day 26 A Beautiful Hike only 14 miles (apx 23k) today...

Giving our body's a chance to recover before we start racking up the miles sliding into home. I thought today was going to be all down hill out of O'Cebreiro but it actually surprised us a little with a mixed bag of; up down and all around, for about the first half of the day, before we plummeted down to Tricastela. But a beautiful hike it was!

We ended up running into Gringo #3 James, in O'cebreiro, so that was a fun treat... He has been pulling some big days (a couple 30 milers) and so we have hop scotched over each other a few times but today we got to walk together into Triacastela.

Look this statue has Tony's sandals on... See he's just being an authentic peregrino :-)

If you can see the little black dots flying behind Tony here.... those are flies.

They're are a lot of cows therefore a lot of flies... no biggie though.

Can you believe how beautiful the view is??? Talk about patchwork...

And to all our Sedona skinny vacationer's... This area gives a whole new meaning to "Cow pies trail" At first I was calling it "poop path" but then I remembered Cow Pies in Sedona and that sounded nicer.

In some of the older, not so commercial villages, there's cow poop everywhere but the cool thing is all the hard working, hardy people, you see working the farms, especially the women.
We were walking yesterday (at the hottest point of the day) and a woman (who had to be around 70) wearing a long denim skirt and carrying a rake taller than she was, came out of the fields.

 The fields were at a steep angle, on the side of the mountain, and as she walked past us I said "hola" and she responded "hola" with the strongest voice. You could tell this woman was tough! It was hot as hell and she's climbing up and down these mountains tending her farm... Awesome!

As promised the trail is getting busier. Today is the first town we have pulled into and been told "completo" or no vacancy, at several places, before settling on Casa of David... a great place with very friendly owners... thank goodness!

And as promised the food in Galicia has been much tastier!! With the exception of us not having any clue what we ordering most of the time.

Today I saw two "house specialty" dishes and thought "Hey I'll try what they're known for" one translated into "soup with vegetables"... and the other a garbanzo bean dish... so they sounded pretty safe. HOWEVER.... when the garbanzo bean dish arrived it was tripe... YIKES!!!! I couldn't even stand the smell of it, sitting on the table in front of me, so I politely waved the waitress over and told her I was very full and to please take it away... Thanks goodness the appetizers; delicious roasted peppers, calamari and vegetable soup were amazing (and filling) so she believed me... I think.

The plan now is to speed up and get this thing done. I have now booked two nights ahead and if our bodies hold up we will do four 20-24 mile days in a row and end up in Santiago Thursday late or Friday early. We plan on speeding up into Santiago and maybe bus to Finisterre or maybe visit Madrid before heading home...

At least that's the plan. Who knows what's to come? On the Camino I've learned...

It's best gifts are it's surprises....Woo Hooooo

Ultreia!

Day 27 I don't recommend doing it this way!

I'm a little delirious so I'm just going to throw up some pictures and tell you my "Luke" story and then fill in more later...

We did the "Tony and Molli Marathon" today and I don't recommend it...

Basically you walk 26 miles, from Triacastela to Portomarin, which takes you like 9 hours because no matter how fast, you *feel,* you're walking your only averaging 3 miles per hour... (I guess because you have a pack on your back or you're in some kind of Camino Vortex)... Add to that you can't figure out where you are on the map so you think you're a lot closer than you are, the entire last half, and then you finish up with lots of hills and 90+ degree weather... good times! Oh and then just to top it off we're planning the same thing again tomorrow.... What?

Yes we're looking to get this baby done ASAP!
So now rather than bore you with stories of today's hike I'll instead give you my "luke" story... "Luke you are my Grasshopper"

Last night we're in this cute place Casa David and in the middle of the day we get in the room and I hear this rattle, very distinct and loud almost like a rattlesnake but quick. So I figure it must be something right outside our window.

The sound stops but every once in awhile I hear it again just for a second. The room is basically a concrete cell... a pretty cell, but a cell nonetheless, so everything echoes and the walls are paper thin. If the guy next door farts we're going to hear it. So again I figure it must be coming from outside.

I hear it again and now I'm creeped out so I start moving desks, etc. Because I'm freaking out there might be a rattlesnake in our room.

Again this is basically impossible because our room is inside two doors and there's barely even a window. But still I move the desk, I pick up bags, etc. trying to find where this sound, which happens about once an hour, is coming from. Meanwhile Tony laughs at me... It's now night time and Tony is drifting off to sleep... I still haven't found the source of the noise I run down all the things that could be making the noise... crickets make weird noises right? But they don't shut up and this one keeps stopping... Rattlesnakes... but then if I bang around it would rattle more because they pick up on your vibration.... ROACHES! Don't roaches make some kind of sound? but only at night and it's not dark and I keep telling myself this place is immaculate.... How about a machine?

Tony falls asleep and I hear it again. This time I about leap out of bed because now it's moved from the far corner of the room to the corner much closer to me. This always happens Tony falls asleep and I'm left freaking out over sounds in the night... this is why I don't camp. So I get up, put on my glasses and find my head lamp.

Yes the first time I've pulled out my headlamp on the Camino is to search for a noise in my hotel room. I realize I haven't looked under the bed yet and now I'm convinced I'm going to see a rattlesnake or roaches under the bed...

but nothing. I search every corner and again the room is pristine and nothing... Tony sleeps on... No noise.

"Ok Molli get over it... It's not a snake so what's the worst that can happen? You wake up in the middle of the night with roaches scurrying about? Get over it!" So I leave the TV on because I think roaches like the dark. This annoys Tony, he wakes up, and he turns it off in the middle of the night..(I don't bother to explain my neurosis) and fall asleep.

About an hour later I feel something tickle my back... I know something is on me and I flick... and grab for my glasses. I can see a figure sitting on top of the sheet.

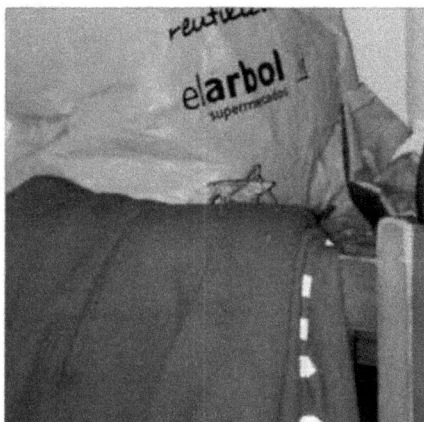

Luckily I don't scream because the guy next door would probably have a heart attack.. Tony wakes up and I say "shhhh... it's sitting right there" and point to the figure. Then we turn on the light and there's "Luke" sitting on top of the sheet.

He's like " Hey, What is there a problem??".... I'm so relieved to finally know the source of my intermittent rattle that he becomes my best friend. We brush him off onto the ground but as I go to sleep I feel bad for not putting him outside because he's trapped in this room. In my head I tell him to be where I can see him in the morning and I'll put him outside.

This morning when I opened my eyes guess where "Luke" was sitting? On top of my sweatshirt right where I couldn't miss him... "Good Luke!" Tony put him safely outside and the day began...

Here are the pics in no particular order...

Lots of really pretty bulls...

Every little village you come into typically has a couple dogs roaming around... They're working farm dogs so they're really cool... This village had a puppy and as we approached he looked like he was playing with a palm frond or something. He was a cutie pie and brought it over to us to play with too... Which we thought was a great idea until we saw it was a chicken's wing...

This is one of the 100k signs

and here's another one about a .25 mile down the road...

Did we mention they're not always real accurate with distances around here?

The best sandwich I think I've ever tasted at Casa Morgade... I must have been really hungry but Damn that was good!

A fun Rastafarian store... No shopping Molli!

This is the point (or town closest to the point) where you're supposed to walk all the way into Santiago or the Compestela police come and find you... or at least we thought this was the town. Turns out it was a little further along than that.

We past several markers that seemed to be "The marker" did I mention some of the distances seem a little off?
The funny thing is we traveled 500 miles across a Country and had distance markers the entire way... That alone is a miracle. They're not vandalized. They're pretty accurate. They're easy to follow. It's amazing... but when you get here, to the end, where the vast majority of people "jump on" they become a little confusing.

But then again... now that I think about it. That's very fitting for the Camino. Another "Camino" Lesson. If you're here to clock the miles are you really here?

And this is the bridge and stairs which take you into Portomarin.... A perfect way to complete a marathon the worst marathon ever wouldn't you say?

Day 28 I felt like a walking zombie

25 miles today Portomarin to Melide (40.2 k)

Tomorrow is the last *real* hiking day... (Woo hoo) 20.5 miles (33k) into Arca tomorrow and then it's only 12 miles into Santiago on Thursday. I think our feet will last exactly that long but not a second further....

We're actually not sore except for the bottom of our poor little feet. We keep trying to talk to them and tell them "We'll stop soon... I promise".

The coolest part about today's hike was that we left in the dark. It was our first night hike... we got up at 5am, and out the door, so we wouldn't be caught in as much heat as yesterday. Anything after 2pm is just excruciatingly hot!

Walking in the dark was pretty freaky but we used our headlamps and our flashlight (Iphone App). It worked out perfectly because coming out of Portomarin was a simple trek, to follow, with no big mistakes you could make. It was just up hill through a forest on a wide dirt path so it was a great day to do it.

And it was definitely our favorite part of the day...

This morning, after yesterday's excruciating hike Tony felt good and I felt like a walking zombie. At one point I looked down at my legs and was pretty amused at how dissociated from them I felt. They seemed to keep walking forward, without a problem, but my head was somewhere completely separate.

Then about 8k in we stopped for breakfast and had fried eggs, potatoes, chorizo, coffee and orange juice and it was like I had just been hooked up to an I.V... I was alive again!

Orange juice (zumo naranja) has been our Savior here. I never drink juice, at home, but here we're having several glasses a day. It's fresh squeezed (right in front of you) and delicious! And it's exactly what you need to perk you up as you go. It only took me 25 days to learn how to order it correctly. I didn't know the word for juice so I would say "naranja" (orange) and they would stare at me blankly and then I would say orange juice and do charades and they got it... Then one of the cafe owners explained to me "zumo" is juice and from then on it's been easy to get.

The hike today was pretty but uneventful... There seemed to be a big fire happening somewhere so we could smell and see the smoke all day.

It took me a couple hours to remember the word for fire (fuego) but once I remembered it I knew it wouldn't matter because if I asked someone I still wouldn't understand anything else they said about it.

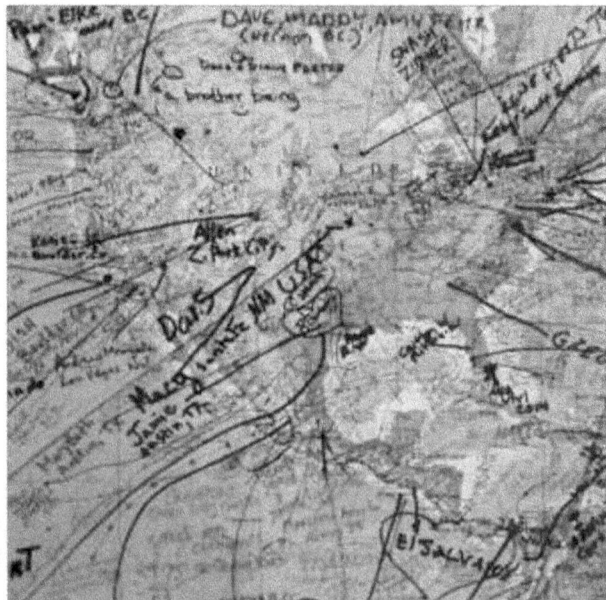

One of the cool cafes we stopped in had this map on the wall.

The other plus today, we didn't go through as many "cow pie villages". Yesterday the hike took us through what the guide books refers to as "hamlets". They are not hamlets... they are cow shit, covered tiny, towns.

Here's how the Camino works they regularly re-route you off the main road and through villages because many villages subsist based on the business the pilgrims bring them. If you pass by on the road, above a village, you might not be inclined to stop. So the arrows (route) takes you directly through the towns.

Sometimes this gets really annoying because you can see a road right next to you which is more direct and say for example flat... where as the arrows might take you a hundred yards up a hill, down a hill, and back up again, only to go through a village.

Yesterday I had, had enough of these re-directions because they kept dropping us down into dairy farms.

Sometimes you even get so lucky you get to wait behind the cows while they pass through. The towns themselves are about 100 yards long and appear to be completely dedicated to dairy farming.

Everyday they walk the cows from the barn, up the middle of the town, to the milking area and out into the fields to graze. Don't get me wrong I have the utmost respect for these people and their way of life. They're hard working and the animals look very well cared for. HOWEVER that does not mean I want to walk through 42 towns, down a hill, and back up the other side of cow shit splattered streets, walls, etc. all while holding my breath, when I could stay on the nice clean road right next to it!!!

I'm sure they would not appreciate walking through my neighborhood over and over again either. One or two, to see the culture, is awesome but not every one... come on!

Today's cow shit villages were a little cleaner, bigger, and more commercial than yesterdays but if today had been a copy of yesterday.... we were taking the road.

I know I know it sounds horrible and I'm an ass for saying it but it's a lot of poop and I'm tired and I'm trying to give you the full picture not just the pretty parts.

This farmer was awesome... he kept trying to tell us this is where cafe con leche comes from. As I said it's a treasure to see, a couple of them, but not every single one.

Speaking of Farm to table... or Sea to table rather... another highlight today was the Pulpo Gallego (boiled octopus).

This is a Galician delicacy and we were excited to try it. As soon as we pulled into Melide, Pulperia Ezequiel, was our first stop.

Here's the octopus boiling in the pots

and then they take it out and chop it up with scissors, cover it with olive oil, paprika and rock salt

and it's all yours...

They serve their wine in ceramic white bowls... Luckily I read this in the guidebook beforehand... otherwise I would have been staring at the white bowls wondering what they were for and why they would not bring me a darn glass so I could drink my wine... ha ha ha.

Almost done.... I think tomorrow will start to feel like a party... The calm aspects of the Camino are long gone... Ultreia!

Day 29 Our last big day

This morning before we left the hotel I affixed a sign with the number 29 written on it to my back pack. I did this because I was starting to get tired of being pushed around by people who had just joined the trail.

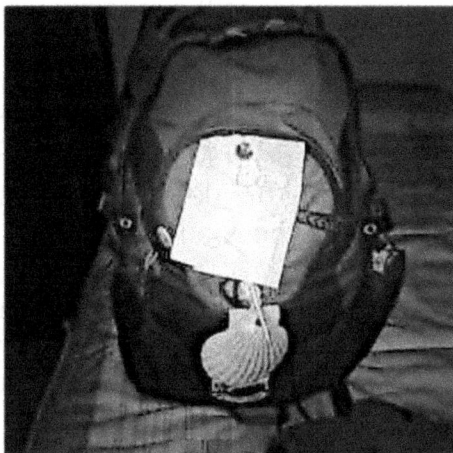

I wanted to provide a not so subtle reminder that some people out here are tired and in a different mental state than those who are making a three day weekend out of their 100k into Santiago.

Think of it this way.. imagine you were doing a full marathon. You're exhausted, you've been running for hours and then just 5k from the finish line fresh runners come in who are only doing a 5k. They're fast vibrant, pushy and totally not doing the same event you're doing so they run you over.

This is how it feels to enter into the last 100km of the Camino, after you've been out there for a month, and this is why I put a note on my back today. Not to be an ass, not to gloat, just to remind people that if I come across a little slow or grumpy... well read the sign.

Today was 20.5 miles (33km). Our last tough day. This portion of the Camino undulates up and down through river valleys as beautiful oak tree groves turn into Eucalyptus forests. Both are stunning!

Tony and I seem to have a knack for being alone on the Camino no matter how busy it is... I don't know if it's our timing or what but we see big packs of people and we always seem to be in a wave between them. Left alone which is how I prefer it. I think it's a gift of the Camino to us. So today even though we have now entered the "busy" section we still primarily walked alone.

Although I remembered to put on my "sign" this morning I failed to remember to pay for our hotel room!!! About 5k outside of Melide Tony and I were sitting at a cafe, enjoying breakfast when I gasped. "Oh My God I forgot to pay for the room last night!"

Here's how this works, when you're staying at the private hotels they graciously check you in when you arrive but they won't let you pay. We found they like to keep their "check ins" and "check outs" separate... but this doesn't really work well for the peregrino because if you leave at the crack of dawn there's no one to check you out.

I would generally beg the hosts to let me pay for the room right then. What usually ended up happening is we would go down in the evening and ask again and then they had no problem but last night I forgot to do that (probably because I was crashed out asleep by 6pm all filled up on white wine and Pulpo but forgot I did).

So there I sat in the cafe horrified! We weren't about to walk back, we didn't dare get in a cab. I can't converse over the phone in Spanish and no one around us could translate.

Because we had reserved the room with a credit card, through hotels.com, we kept thinking surely they'll be able to charge that card. But something kept nagging at me that we better get a hold of them. So I called and called and got disconnected several times and spoke very broken Spanish to the wonderful woman at the front desk She was very patient and apologetic and I kept saying I was so sorry and she kept saying she was so sorry but I could tell it was very important that I call and she probably would have been in a lot of trouble if I hadn't taken care of the bill.

I can't describe how hysterical it was to listen to me trying to give a credit card number in Spanish over the phone "Cuatro no no no I mean cinco" you see for me to count in Spanish I have to start from the beginning and count on my fingers because I have it memorized as more of a song than actually knowing what they mean.

Uno, dos, tres, cuatro, cinco...

if I don't say them all together I don't know them (Pathetic I know! We didn't call ourselves "gringos" for nothing) and so an hour later and several calls back and forth (once we figured out she was needing an expiration date not the security code) I successfully paid for our room. Between the cost for the room and the cost of an hour on the phone I'm pretty sure it ended up being a really expensive night!

My sign fell off part way through the day... which was fine. I got over myself.

Entering Arca (also known as Pedrouzo... be careful some towns are known by more than one name so keep your eye out for that it can get confusing). Speaking of confusing... as we entered Arca we got a little lost finding our lodging for the night. There is nothing more frustrating than being exhausted, thinking you're done with your walk for the day, and then having to walk around lost because you can't find your albergue.

You just want to sit down, cry, and say "I'm not taking one more step, in any direction, if I don't know EXACTLY where I'm going".

But we found it and this ended up being our favorite night on the entire Camino.

The people who own this private hostel are lovely. It is also their home and we sat with them for hours talking broken Spanglish. The father and Tony really hit it off.

He wanted to know all about earthquakes in California and we of course wanted to know everything. Their 18yr old son joined us part way through the evening and started translating for us but I think Tony and the dad were having more fun figuring each other out.

The love of this family literally brought me to tears because I could see the respect and deep appreciation they had for each other. When was the last time you sat at a table with your teenage children, without a television on, or a phone in anyone's hand, you just sat and talked for hours? I asked the boy if he didn't have something else he'd rather be doing and he looked at me perplexed and said he loved spending time with his parents.

That night is a moment in time I will never forget. A connection, a meal, a conversation which was more charades than words.

Watching Tony and the father talk, I learned if two people are willing to slow down, and listen with their hearts, you probably don't need a common language to communicate what you're trying to convey...

It was a true Camino gift.

Day 30 Sliding into Home

I'll fill in the blanks later when I'm more coherent but we're heeeerrrrreee!!!!!! Santiago Baby!

Leaving Arca, this morning, we immediately started walking through more Eucalyptus forests and I stopped, at one point, to take a photo. I wanted to catch the beauty of what I was seeing and how pretty the light looked coming through the trees.

When I put the camera up to my eyes it was as if I had caught a freeway system of spirits in the lens. It was a dull rainbow of lights flashing about, so fast, you can't even imagine! I gasped (and at least remembered to take the shot) before I pulled the camera away from face to see if I catch what I was seeing, with my naked eye... but no it was gone and when I put the camera back up to my eye it was no longer there.

I was overwhelmed with a feeling of Joy. That the spirits, angels, guardians, past camino walkers were all here... all celebrating and protecting the remainder of everyone's journey. It was pure magic.

We were not alone.... The spirits were dancing in this forest... It was a celebration!

The Camino is a beautiful place... beneath all the tourism and commercialism it's still there. But that's true with all of life right? There is so much crap to keep us distracted, and our egos going, a mile a minute but if you listen, hard enough, the Camino, God, the Universe (whatever you believe speaks to you) is always there. We just have to listen quietly and closely... pay attention. The beauty is there in every day life... in every moment... not only here.

We had breakfast in what felt like a very commercial cafeteria sort of place. It's jarring to have the Camino change so much so quickly. It went from feeling like a serene paradise to feeling like the busiest day, in Disneyland, pretty much over night.

Sitting at the cafe, we looked over and a man waved us over. He looked vaguely familiar, to me, but Tony knew right away.

The man thanked Tony profusely and said how much the exercises Tony had taught him back in Ages (Day 12) had helped him complete his dream of doing the Camino.

Ok seriously people if you had any idea of how packed this place was and the likelihood of running into this person at this hour of the morning, whom we hadn't seen since Day 12... It's impossible! But God is not impossible.

While we all chatted a woman came over and said she overheard our American accents and that we had been on the Camino since St Jean. She was dumbfounded and completely in awe of our accomplishments.

She was fulfilling a life long dream, of hers, by doing the last 100km into Santiago. She felt the journey had been very strenuous and couldn't believe we had been out there for a month.

We met several people like this during the final 100k... Seeing her excitement I realized how important it was not to make light of anyone's journey on the Camino, no matter the distance. She was probably more excited and proud of herself, for what she accomplished, than we were for what we had just done.

I knew at that moment everyone who walks into the square, in Santiago, is equal and to never judge what someone's journey may or may not have meant to them. The distance has nothing to do with it.

It's a celebration for all!

I left the cafe with a renewed sense of wonder for the Camino.

The Kilometers have been painstakingly marked for the entire 776 K journey but in the last ten km... what do you know... NO marks at all... I got the "impression" this was going to happen and so we made up our own as we counted down our last 10k into Santiago. (See blog for our own personal countdown into Santiago)...

Then you reach the City of Santiago and you still have about 5k more to walk before you get to the Cathedral (which I think might be why they don't mark this area's distance)...

And then we arrived...

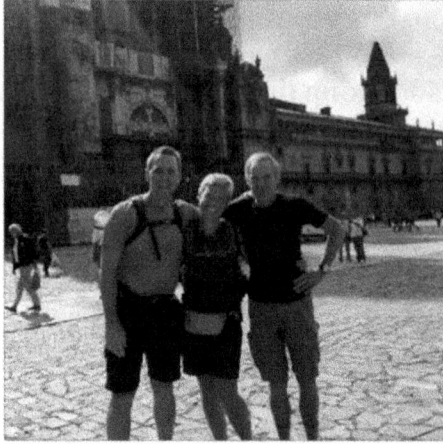

The City is beautiful...

The Cathedral is stunning...

It did not disappoint construction and all.

And guess who found us in the square?

William from Ireland... Do you remember William from Day 3 Pamplona?

He had walked the Camino all the way from Ireland and at that point was at week 6...

Well he had walked to Finisterre and back and is now here with his wife. That is the magic of the Camino...

We haven't seen William since Day 3 and here we are ending up a couple days early and we run into him in the Square... the probability of that is basically impossible.

But God is not impossible.

And James? Well James decided to pull some crazy miles and ended up in Santiago last night. He is headed on to Finisterre. We found out through facebook Adam ended up completing the task about a week behind us...

The Holland Couple showed up the next day and we were lucky enough to share one more dinner and ice cream with them before we parted. We ended up at the same church service as The Folsom couple and the mom and daughter team from Napa and we even got to see Michael one last time. But we never did find out if "Alaska" made it... I hope you did girl!

So a happy ending for all...

In Brierley's book, on reflecting on Santiago, he has this passage which I find beautiful...

"As I entered the Cathedral I realized I had failed in my purpose. But in that same instant I realized I had been searching in the wrong place. A sudden rush of joy enveloped my soaking body. I knew the answer lay where the world of things ended and the unseen world began and I knew I had to go there. I hurried down the steps and out the city. I was alone but I had company. I did not know where I was going but I felt completely guided."

As for Tony and I were are eternally, and overwhelmingly, grateful for the experience. We are very much looking forward to leaving the arrows behind and finding our own way.

The journey is always within....

We wish you, all, your very own and the best of

Buen Caminos!

Final Takeaways...

These pics are literally the first moment we saw the dogs... God I missed them!

Since coming home and connecting with friends and family there are two main questions we've been asked the first is;

"Did you get out of it what you were hoping to?"

The answer is unequivocally "Yes". We went in search of an adventure. I went because it called to both my husband, and me, both before we were married and after.

I went to find a closer, clearer, connection to God and yes I feel more deeply led now than at any other point in my life.

There is something about the Camino. I have no idea why, that spot on the planet, but there is something going on there that is more than this physical world.

It's cloaked in the commercialism and reality of everyday life so when you first arrive you are a little caught off guard, at least I was, because I guess you have an expectation that you will be able to see the difference right away, and you can't because it's not of this world. Your ego mind can't see any difference....

You have to shut up, turn within, and listen and then it's there like an alternate universe, a different dimension. It starts talking and working on you almost immediately. I can imagine many people go there and experience nothing of what I'm talking about because if you don't quiet your mind, you won't. You could be so busy that you could miss ALL of the messages, gifts, lessons, God and your Angels are sending you.

I heard many people, there, having the same conversations they would have had around a board room, at home, and I had to wonder

"If you came here to have the same conversation you would have had at work. Why are you here?"

But this is true in everyday life as well. God is always there we just keep saying "we're too busy to listen".

I don't know why the Camino... maybe people are called there to get closer to God and then come home and spread the light. I'm not sure what we're tapping into there but if you have been called I wouldn't ignore it ...

Which leads me to the second thing we've been asked

"Would you recommend doing the trip?"...

We believe everyone who walks the Camino will have a completely unique experience. That may sound obvious to you "Well of course they will. Two people can never experience the same exact thing." but here it goes deeper than that.

One of the gifts of the Camino is its ability to transmute itself into a completely different experience for each soul walking it. You see this as you meet and talk with people at the end of each day.

On about Day 22 we caught up with one of the friends we had made on Day 2 in Zubiri... it had been awhile since we had seen her and we recanted our experiences so far... it was as if we were on two entirely different trips. Listening to the two of us tell our tales you would have never imagined we had been to the same place.

She had stayed with the group of twenty something's we had swum with, in the river, in Zubiri. They had become a close, fun, group and two of the members were camping so they had spent a few of the nights camping with them.

The rest of her stays were in large albergues... bunk beds... public showers/bathrooms. They had swum in many rivers and there was a dog, hiking with one of the guys, so they generally stayed away from the restaurants and more commercial areas and often cooked their own food. One night in Hospital de Orbige the hospitelaros of her albergue drove them to a party in the fields. A bunch of locals were getting together to celebrate the summer solstice and the party as you can imagine was quite the bash... Bonfires, moonshine, etc, etc...

Compare her trip to ours

We swam two times, once in a Spa... Ate in only restaurants... walked alone... The vast majority of the nights we stayed in private hotel rooms with our own shower, bathroom, etc.

So you can see not just spiritually but physically the Camino can be very different things to each person walking the same route.

It reminds me of the old analogy of the blind people and the elephant. Take five people, blind fold them, and have each one touch a different part of an elephant. One person is holding an ear, another the tail, another the broad side of the body, another the trunk, another the foot and have them each describe what they're feeling and try to get the other to experience the same thing and you can't. You're not on the same page.

This is the Camino. My experience will be nothing like your experience. That is one thing I'm sure of...

It gives *you* what you need... It will create unique obstacles for *you* that will only get under *your* skin but wouldn't bother me at all. Like the overly talkative people who drove me nuts and you probably wouldn't even notice.

It will give you gifts that will be precious to you... like the red poppies were to me.

There's no escaping it... your angels know exactly what you need. So much so that you just have to laugh. "Really guys... really?"

So one of our main takeaways is to expect a unique experience and expect both good and bad. There will be gifts and lessons. The gifts will be wonderful but the lessons are VERY hard to swallow.

I immediately came back and in my ego mind I wanted to tell you/anyone how you could "make the trip better"...

"oh just do the first two weeks and then drive to Leon and walk from there... cut out all the yucky parts". "Do this day cut out that day".

I wanted to tell you exactly how YOU *should* do it because *I* was smarter than the Camino and the millions of people who have been walking it since the beginning of time.

God what an idiot I am... but luckily I caught myself and realized a huge lesson. I wanted to protect you from experiencing anything "negative". I wanted to wrap that trip up, shorten it, extract out only the amazing bits.

Modify it to give you only the picture perfect wonderful parts. Tell you exactly what day to be where and how to eat and what to wear and how long to move... and that is where I would have been totally wrong and done you a horrible disservice.

Life is about balance... it's about good and bad... Learning to turn inward... Learning to listen to your inner voice... Learning to feel God is always there for you. And without adversity you don't learn, you don't grow.

I could cry at the thought of how many times I have not been brave enough to allow things to be uncomfortable for myself as well as for others. That's weak and I will take that lesson very seriously.

If the Camino has called to you then yes I would say go but if it hasn't I wouldn't force it. Maybe you have just happened upon this book, or blog, and this is the first your hearing about the Camino. In that case or in the case of people who want to go but just can't get the logistics figured out right now I would say this...

The Camino is always with you... You don't have to go anywhere to find God. Just turn within. Stop saying "you don't have time" to quiet your mind. Devote ten minutes, a half hour, an hour a day to walking, quietly, in Nature.

Take no humans (with the exception of a baby in a stroller if need be). A dog is fine. Animals and babies help us connect. Don't run, walk. It's not a workout, it's an active meditation. A devotion of 1 hour a day to turning within and telling God you have time to listen.

Then Shut up!

Allow the messages to come throughout the day... allow life to be different.

Because of the way our minds work all change is a threat and so often times God sends you the answer but you reject it because of the fear of change. Because the ego portion of our minds keeps trying to convince us that it knows how to keep us safe and that it's got it all figured out.

Allow... allow... allow things to be different. Have faith that you don't always have the answer. That feeling of surrender is where the answers lie.

I love you and thank you for following our journey. It has been as deeply gratifying to write about it as many of you have told us it was to read.

If you do walk the Camino one thing that was recommended to me and I will now pass on to you... is to journal, write, blog your daily experiences. Partly because the whole thing goes so fast it's hard to remember where you've been.

Think about it a different hotel, city, village, every night for 30+ nights your brain really starts to spin and you quickly lose track and sense of what you're doing. It's calming to go back over the day's experiences each evening.

The other reason is that I believe the people who do have the opportunity to walk it have a responsibility of sharing their experience but that was just part of our journey maybe not true for you...

You'll know if it's true for you...

Logistics

Clothes and Packing

The rule of thumb for lots of hikers, including us, is to not let your back pack exceed 10% of your weight.

I think mine weighed in at 13 lbs and Tony's was 21 when we started on the Camino

We started with the following items:

- Back Packs
- Bladders for our camelbaks for water
- 2 Guide books
- Me 2 pair of shoes one trail running shoe, one sandal
- Tony- Luna Sandals and Vibram FiveFingers
- 1 pair shorts each
- 1pair sweats
- 1 pair hiking pants each
- 2 sweat shirts
- 2 Rain jackets
- 2 rain ponchos
- 2 t-shirts Tony
- 2 synthetic shirts Me
- Me one "cute outfit" (lost on Day 10)
- 1 comb
- 1 gallon ziploc bag full of travel size toiletries
- 1 small bottle Dr. Bonner's peppermint soap
- 1 pair glasses, contact lenses and back up pair of lenses
- 2 quick drying camping towels
- 2 pairs toe socks (life savers)
- 2 tennis balls, in one sock, for massage of aching muscles
- 2 very thin sleeping bags
- 2 travel money belts (very handy)
- passports, money, credit cards
- 2 pilgrim's passports
- 2 sunglasses (lost both, bought new ones in Burgos)
- 2 hats
- 1 Ipad
- 1 portable typing keyboard
- 2 smartphones (we did not bring a camera I used my phone)

I think that's about it... by the end, we ended up with just what you see on the bed including our electronics Even thinking we had packed very light, to begin with, we still ended up ditching a lot of stuff along the way.

The Camino has a way of "stripping you down" so even if you think you packed light be prepared to lose more!

Things we were really glad we had included:

The ziploc plastic bag for our toiletries. You have to carry your stuff in and out of communal showers and you need a bag that will dry quickly.

The money belts were handy because we wore them pretty much every second of the 30 days. You can't really leave stuff behind if you're sleeping in a dorm style room. No matter how awesome your bunk mates are!

I found the toe socks to be very helpful in stopping blisters. In fact I had one blister the entire trip. Day 2 and that was the only day I didn't wear toe socks. The brand we use is Injinji . You can get them online or at any good hiking store.

Tony had no blisters. He wore his "Jesus Sandals" 95% of the time and although he got a lot of strange looks, from people, he was very happy with his decision to go for it and use the sandals. I want to stress this though he has been wearing minimalist style shoes for years so please make sure you don't jump right in with a shoe like this. Just like anything else it takes training and you've got to build up your feet to being strong enough to handle a minimalist shoe, then we love them!

Washing machines are hard to come by and electric dryers are VERY scarce so many times you are washing your clothes, by hand, and hanging them to dry. This means two things you want a comfortable outfit to change into while your hiking clothes are getting clean and you need clothes that will dry quickly.

Make sure your back pack is comfortable. Train in it with the weight you think you'll be carrying so you know it works well for you before you go...

In fact train in everything! Your shoes, your socks, your clothes. It's an old athletes secret but even chafing underwear can make you or break you. Train in everything! You want as few surprises as possible because trust me the Camino is going to have surprises all it's own. At least you can be comfortable as you take them on!

Things we didn't use:

I wore no makeup at all... even in Paris :-(

It was warm when we went so Rain Ponchos and jackets were redundant, so one or the other should suffice in summer time, however a poncho big enough to keep your back pack dry or a back pack rain cover is essential. We bought $10 ponchos on Amazon and they worked out perfectly.

The weather can fluctuate greatly so be prepared for your forecasted weather. The hot is HOT and the cold is COLD...

We ended up staying primarily in private hostels so sleeping bags were unnecessary and even many larger albergues provided linens as well.

We did not use our camelbak bladders for water. We ended up sending those home because we found it more convenient to fill up plastic water bottles along the way.

Water is safe for drinking (signage will tell you) and plentiful just make sure you use designated drinking fountains (clearly marked along the way). The tap water was delicious... I never thought I'd encounter that coming from Southern California! Just be sure to fill up as you leave each village and KNOW your mileage!

Companions, as you plan your trip you may start getting insecure and thinking you need buddies to go along with you. Our original thought was "the more the merrier".

We even thought we would one day turn it into one of the adventures we would take our clients on. But after having done it I no longer think that's appropriate, for me, at least.

Don't be afraid to go it alone.

The Camino is a solitary journey, a journey within and you'll meet many friends along the way. Let it take you where it needs to... and if you do decide to bring a friend, spouse, partner, let them have their space.

The Camino has an interesting way of bringing out the best and worst, in all of us, so be kind!

Getting physically prepared for the Camino

The night we met up again with Leah (from Zubiri) and got to hear how her adventures had gone so far we also had dinner with a married couple from the Yukon. They were struggling quite a bit. This was all a little too much for them. Although physically active at home they were completely unprepared for this amount of walking and this heat.

Her body was covered in heat rash and they were both sun burnt. Some of this could have been easily avoided. They admitted themselves they kept leaving far too late in the day and walking too late into the hot afternoons.

According to them there was some kind of "drama" going on at home and they had to keep attending to their son's girlfriend over the phone, each morning, causing them to leave around 10am each day. Hmmmm... It's interesting to watch the traps people get themselves into (it wasn't just me↗). Here they could see a resolution to at least a portion of their problem. Get up early 5:30 am (like pretty much everyone else) and get your butt on that trail!

This helps to ensure you won't be walking past 2:00pm and into the hottest part of the day.

But they couldn't / wouldn't cut that tie with the drama going on at home... Sounds like a Camino lesson to me. The other part of their issue isn't easily resolved out there. During dinner they mentioned how overwhelmed they were becoming by how physically challenging the walks were and how they felt the guidebooks had not done a good enough job portraying the difficulty and physical fitness required to do the Camino.

I had been waiting for somebody to mention this... I am in awe of how the guidebooks brush over the physical fitness required to walk 12+ miles a day (over 19km) for 34 days in a row.

I tried to explain it away...

- "well I guess if you are the type of person who would consider walking across a Country they (the guidebook authors) figure you know what you're in for"
- "maybe people from the rest of the world walk a heck of a lot more than Americans"

One of Tony's explanations made a lot of sense... he thought because for most people this is still a spiritual pilgrimage and "they believe the physical pain or penance is part of the process". Essentially they think "it has to hurt".

Hmmm..... I'm not going to tell you what to think. Your journey is entirely your journey but I will tell you my opinion as a physical fitness expert... Get prepared!

I am an athlete and I still hurt.... If God wants you to hurt to get a message through to you, you'll hurt. God doesn't need the help of you also being an idiot by not preparing yourself to make it through the journey you say you want to go on.

That's like a teenager saying they want to drive but not bothering to take the time to learn just jumping in the car. Or saying you want to be a Doctor when you grow up and not bothering to go to school...

If you claim you want to do something, and you have the time, take the actions required, at home, to prepare yourself. Otherwise your just day dreaming about some romanticized version of yourself that doesn't exist.

Walk today...

Tony and I prepared by walking 10 miles a day, several days a week, on top of our normal physical fitness routines. As we progressed we added weighted back packs.

We hike at high elevation regularly and so days like Day 1, the hike over the Pyrenees, and Day 25 up to O'Cebreiro were completely doable for us.

Please understand and I'm saying this with all caps and underlined for a reason THERE ARE SOME VERY HARD DAYS ON THE CAMINO these hikes are "No Joke!".

They can be broken up... They can be done intelligently (i.e. not 4 o'clock in the afternoon)... and they NEED to be prepared for.

Part of training for any endurance event (which this is) is getting your clothing, gear and shoes figured out. We explain this to our marathon runners all the time.

Part of the time spent training is to figure out which clothes work for you and which do not... The same goes for your shoes.... Socks (very important) and in the case of hiking, your back pack.

This can only be done by walking and putting in miles with the items you will be wearing.

I am always dumbfounded by the people who show up with shoes they haven't spent much time in and new gear... If you want to suffer, that's how to do it!

Everything from your underwear down to how short your toenails are clipped needs to be addressed before taking on a distance of this magnitude.

The amount we suffered was nothing compared to what you see out there. And many, many, people are forced to stop.. quit the Camino as a result of not being prepared.

As in the case of the Yukon couple I mentioned earlier. They were checking out... headed back to the Louvre in Paris. The Camino had turned out to be too much for them.

If you are considering doing the Camino and would like help in your preparation feel free to contact us we're happy to help.

Or if you are sitting at home thinking the Camino might be a little too much for you right now but are ready to start your own journey at home... we'd be happy to help with that as well.

Contact us and start walking!

The Rules

As I mentioned this sometimes feels like a giant scavenger hunt across Spain. You follow "clues", the arrows, collecting stamps for your "Pilgrim passport", (aka The Credencial).

The Pilgrim passport is a certificate (booklet seen in this photo) issued by the Cathedral of Santiago, Camino authorities and volunteer associations along the route which certifies the genuine pilgrim status of the bearer, i.e., that he or she is traveling to Compostela on foot, by bicycle or on horseback.

You can order your Pilgrim Passport in advance of leaving and have it shipped to your home or in our case we picked ours up in St Jean Pied de Port because our hospitalero promised they had them available for us.

Pilgrims have their credenciales stamped at least once each day

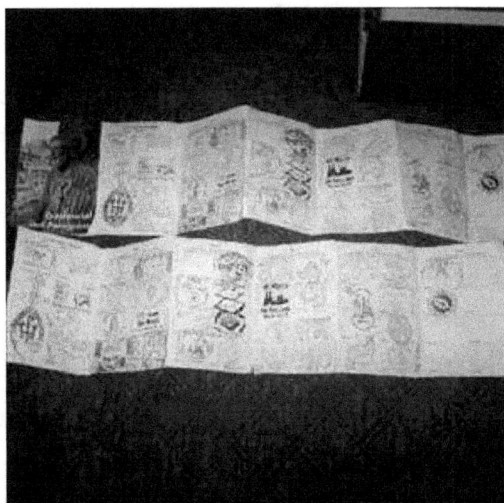

At points all along the route in order to certify that their journey to Compostela meets the conditions required by the Pilgrim Office, at the cathedral, for the granting of the Compostela.

You are also required to show your Pilgrim Passport in order to get access to pilgrim's albergues all along the route so the Pilgrims Passport is very important.

Upon arrival in Santiago de Compostela, pilgrims present the completed credencial at the Pilgrim Office in Santiago, fill in a questionnaire about why they have made the pilgrimage and may then qualify for a Compostela certificate.

Now here's the tricky part... To receive your Compostela, (certificate of completion) you only have to walked the last 100k (62 miles) into Santiago. The "rules" require that at this point you have done so by foot with no vehicular back up or if you are on a bike you must do the last 200k.

(Please note.... I have also read Pilgrims doing only the last 100k must get two stamps a day so please verify this. Don't use the info on this blog as your only source... we're just a pair of gringos and don't want to mess up your trip!)

We keep being warned the last 100k becomes a mad house. From Sarria on busses of people are dropped off to do the last 100k into Santiago making getting a room at night very difficult. Many of the pilgrims we have spoken with have booked all of their accommodations from Sarria on in advance.

All of this is to receive your Compostela...

There are two documents which pilgrims may receive upon arrival at the Cathedral in Santiago: one is the Compostela, a document written in Latin which confirms the completion of pilgrimages undertaken for religious devotion (pietatis causa) or an attitude of spiritual searching in which one is at least open to faith in God.

The other is a certificado, or certificate, confirming completion of the journey by those pilgrims who have undertaken the journey for recreational motives, i.e., a holiday or as a physical challenge.

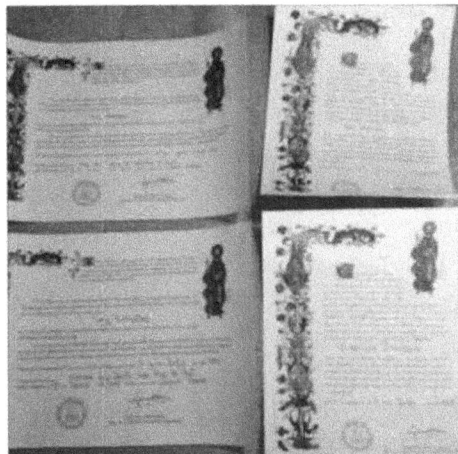

The Compestela is written in Latin. Below is the English translation of the text of the Compostela:

"The Chapter of this Holy, Apostolic, Metropolitan Cathedral of St. James, custodian of the seal of St. James' Altar, to all faithful and pilgrims who come from everywhere over the world as an act of devotion, under vow or promise to the Apostle's Tomb, our Patron and Protector of Spain, witnesses in the sight of all who read this document, that: Mr/Mrs....................has visited devoutly this Sacred Church in a religious sense (pie causa). Witness whereof I hand this document over to him, authenticated by the seal of this Sacred Church. Given in St. James de Compostela on the (day)...... (month)......A.D. .... Chapter Secretary" Apart from the devotional or religious motives mentioned above, pilgrims must have completed at least the last 100km on foot without interruption in order to qualify (cyclists must do the last 200 km).

As I understand it upon arrival in Compostela, the pilgrim must take his or her credencial, or Pilgrim Passport, to the Pilgrim Office near the cathedral. Where you stand in line and are asked about the motivation for your pilgrimage, and, once the authorities are satisfied that the conditions for the pilgrimage have been satisfied, the Compostela is issued.

Got all that? Phew! They may lose us a little here. We came, we saw, we experienced... I'm not sure I need a piece of paper to verify what I already know. We'll see how long the line is... :-)

We've been told at the high end of the season something like 1500 people a day receive their Compostela. We haven't even seen 1500 people on the trail yet so I can't fathom what this is about to change into, if that's true.

Stay in the Now...

Muchas Gracias!

The Camino is indeed a mystical place. The mystery lies on levels beneath the surface. On the surface we see a beautiful Country with the typical problems, we all face; torn by politics, pride, economy. Nonetheless Spain is vibrant, proud and intact.

I believe the mystical side, of the Camino, is only possible because Spain has done such a beautiful job of making, and keeping, the Camino accessible.

I have never seen another spot on the planet where you can walk 500 miles (or more) with village after village and town after town accommodating you along the way.
For the most part we were welcomed in to homes, churches, restaurants and towns with open arms.

Where else in the world would you feel safe enough to WALK and trust thousands of, painted yellow, arrows to mark your way? It is only because you are able to put your mind at rest and trust the arrow will be there, the bed will be there, and the food will be there, that you are able to dive deep within and allow the Camino to work its magic.

And for this I am eternally grateful... Viva España!

El Camino es un lugar místico y su encanto se encuentra bajo la superficie. A pura vista aparenta ser un lugar hermoso que, como tantos otros, suelen ser afectados por los diluvios de la humanidad... politica, economía y orgullo. Sin embargo, esta parte de España logra mantenerse vibrante, honrada e intacta.

Yo creo que el Camino Místico solo puede existir gracias a la gente de España que permite que esta parte del territorio sea accesible a todo extranjero y patriota que desee travesarlo.

Jamás he visto algún otro lugar en el planeta en el cual uno pueda caminar mas de mil quilómetros con tanta gente y albergues dispuestos a darnos la bienvenida y proveernos con casa y comida.

En que otro lugar en el mundo existe el lujo de haber un camino con miles de millas regadas de flechas amarillas apuntando donde seguir en el cual uno no necesita preocuparse de ser atacado y en el cual uno puede tener fe que al llegar a cada paraje uno va a tener acceso a comida, cama, y techo? Solo en estas circunstancias el Camino puede lograr brindarnos su magia.

Por esta oportunidad, le estoy eternamente agradecida...

Viva España!

www.ingramcontent.com/pod-product-compliance
Lightning Source LLC
Chambersburg PA
CBHW060301100426
42742CB00011B/1830